Contents

Copyrights

Transformative Leadership in Pharmaceutical Sales: Strategies for Success in Life Sciences

ISBN: [9798328021531]

First Edition: 2024

Publisher: Amazon Kindle

For more information, visit https://www.linkedin.com/in/tarek-mansour/

Introduction

In the dynamic and highly competitive world of pharmaceutical sales, success requires more than just an understanding of the market. It demands visionary leadership, innovative strategies, and the ability to navigate a rapidly evolving landscape. This book, **"Transformative Leadership in Pharmaceutical Sales: Strategies for Success in Life Sciences,"** is designed to equip you with the tools, insights, and strategies needed to excel in this challenging environment.

Why This Book?

The pharmaceutical industry is at a crossroads. Traditional sales tactics are no longer sufficient to meet the demands of an increasingly complex market. Healthcare providers are more informed and discerning, regulatory requirements are stricter, and the competition is fiercer than ever. To thrive in this environment, sales managers must evolve, adopting new approaches that leverage technology, prioritize ethical practices, and focus on customer-centric strategies.

This book draws on my extensive experience in the pharmaceutical sector, including over 16 years in various strategic roles at AstraZeneca. My journey has taught me invaluable lessons about leadership, innovation, and resilience. I have seen firsthand the transformative power of effective leadership and the impact it can have on a team, a company, and ultimately, on patient outcomes.

Who Is This Book For?

Whether you are a seasoned sales leader, an aspiring manager, or a professional in the pharmaceutical industry looking to enhance your skills, this book is for you. It offers practical insights and actionable strategies that can be applied across different roles and functions within the industry. By following the journey of Sarah, a fictional yet relatable sales manager, you will gain a deeper understanding of how to implement these strategies in real-world scenarios.

What to Expect

Each chapter of this book delves into a critical aspect of pharmaceutical sales management. You will learn how to:

- Develop visionary leadership and strategic planning skills.
- Build a customer-centric culture that enhances satisfaction and loyalty.
- Navigate the complex regulatory landscape with confidence.
- Foster a culture of innovation and continuous improvement.
- Develop resilience and adaptability to thrive in a VUCA (Volatile, Uncertain, Complex, and Ambiguous) world.
- Leverage technology to enhance sales performance.
- Strengthen relationships with key stakeholders.
- Promote diversity and inclusion within your team.
- Integrate sustainability and corporate social responsibility into your strategy.
- Lead through change and uncertainty with grace and effectiveness.

Real-Life Applications

Throughout the book, you will find real-life examples, case studies, and practical templates that illustrate successful strategies and best practices. These tools are designed to help you implement the concepts discussed and drive significant impact in your organization.

A Journey of Continuous Learning

The pharmaceutical industry is constantly evolving, and so must we. This book is not just a one-time read but a guide that you can return to as you continue your journey of learning and development. The strategies and insights shared here are meant to inspire you to think differently, challenge the status quo, and strive for excellence in every aspect of your role.

Final Thoughts

Transformative leadership is about more than achieving sales targets; it's about making a meaningful impact on the lives of patients, advancing health equity, and fostering a culture of innovation and integrity. As you embark on this journey, I encourage you to embrace the challenges, celebrate the successes, and continuously seek opportunities for growth and improvement.

Welcome to **"Transformative Leadership in Pharmaceutical Sales: Strategies for Success in Life Sciences."** Let's begin this journey together.

Chapter 1: Introduction to Pharmaceutical Sales Management

The Journey Begins

In the bustling city of New York, Sarah J. sat at her desk, contemplating the next steps in her career. As a seasoned sales representative in the pharmaceutical industry, she had been on the front lines, engaging with healthcare providers, understanding their needs, and ensuring that her company's products reached the patients who needed them most. Now, an exciting opportunity had presented itself: the chance to step into a managerial role. This promotion wasn't just a testament to her hard work; it was a new challenge, one that required a deeper understanding of the pharmaceutical industry and a fresh set of skills.

Sarah remembered her early days in sales, filled with excitement and trepidation. She had quickly learned that the pharmaceutical industry was unique—complex, regulated, and constantly evolving. Her success depended not only on her ability to sell but also on her understanding of the intricate web of stakeholders involved in healthcare. Now, as she prepared to take on a leadership role, she knew she needed to revisit these fundamentals with a broader perspective.

The Pharmaceutical Industry Landscape

To understand her new role, Sarah began by revisiting the basics. The pharmaceutical industry is vast, encompassing everything from drug discovery and development to manufacturing, marketing, and sales. It operates under stringent regulations to ensure the safety, efficacy, and quality of medicines.

She visualized the drug development process—a long, arduous journey from the laboratory to the patient's bedside. It all starts with **drug discovery**, where researchers identify potential compounds that could become new medicines. This phase is followed by **preclinical testing**, where these compounds are tested in the lab and on animals to assess their safety and biological activity. Only a fraction of these compounds make it to the next stage: **clinical trials**.

Phases of Clinical Trials:

1. **Phase I**: Tests on a small group of healthy volunteers to evaluate safety and dosage.
2. **Phase II**: Tests on a larger group of patients to assess efficacy and side effects.
3. **Phase III**: Tests on a much larger patient population to confirm effectiveness, monitor side effects, and compare the drug to commonly used treatments.

Once a drug successfully passes all three phases, the company can file for regulatory approval. In the United States, this means submitting a New Drug Application (NDA) to the Food and Drug Administration (FDA). After approval, the drug enters the **market** phase, where Sarah's role as a sales manager becomes crucial.

The Role of a Sales Manager

As Sarah prepared for her new role, she outlined the core responsibilities of a pharmaceutical sales manager. This position was about more than just overseeing sales; it was about being a leader, a strategist, and a mentor.

Key Responsibilities of a Pharmaceutical Sales Manager:

1. **Leadership and Team Management**: Leading a team of sales representatives, providing guidance, support, and motivation. Building a cohesive team that works towards common goals.

2. **Strategic Planning**: Developing and implementing sales strategies to meet or exceed sales targets. Analyzing market trends, competitor activities, and customer needs to adjust strategies as necessary.

3. **Customer Relationship Management**: Building and maintaining strong relationships with healthcare providers,

understanding their needs, and ensuring they have the information and support they need.

4. **Compliance and Ethical Practices**: Ensuring all sales activities comply with industry regulations and company policies. Promoting ethical behavior and integrity within the team.

5. **Training and Development**: Providing ongoing training and development opportunities for sales representatives to enhance their skills and knowledge.

Sarah realized that her new role required a balance of tactical and strategic thinking. She would need to be hands-on with her team while also keeping an eye on the bigger picture. One of the most important aspects of her job would be to ensure that her team was not only meeting their sales targets but also doing so in a way that aligned with the company's values and regulatory requirements.

The Complex Web of Stakeholders

In the pharmaceutical industry, sales managers must navigate a complex web of stakeholders, each with their own needs, motivations, and challenges. Sarah mapped out the key players she would need to engage with:

Key Stakeholders in Pharmaceutical Sales:

1. **Healthcare Providers (HCPs)**: Doctors, nurses, and pharmacists are the primary customers. They rely on accurate, up-to-date information about products to make informed decisions for their patients.

2. **Patients**: Ultimately, the end-users of pharmaceutical products. Understanding patient needs and experiences can help tailor sales strategies.

3. **Regulatory Bodies**: Organizations like the FDA in the US or the EMA in Europe ensure that all marketing and sales activities comply with stringent regulations.

4. **Internal Teams**: Collaborating with marketing, compliance, and medical affairs teams to ensure a cohesive approach.

5. **Payers**: Insurance companies and government programs that determine which drugs are covered and at what cost. Engaging with these stakeholders is critical for market access.

The Evolving Market Dynamics

Sarah knew that the pharmaceutical market was constantly evolving. Factors such as technological advancements, regulatory changes, and shifting patient demographics all played a role in shaping the industry. She identified several key trends:

Key Trends in the Pharmaceutical Industry:

1. **Digital Transformation**: The rise of digital tools and platforms has transformed how sales teams interact with healthcare providers and patients. Virtual meetings, webinars, and digital marketing campaigns have become the norm. Embracing digital channels can enhance engagement and provide valuable insights through data analytics.

2. **Personalized Medicine**: Advances in genomics and biotechnology have led to the development of personalized therapies tailored to individual patients. This requires a more nuanced approach to sales and marketing. Sales managers need to be well-versed in these new therapies and able to communicate their benefits effectively.

3. **Value-Based Healthcare**: There is a growing emphasis on value-based healthcare, where the focus is on outcomes rather than volume. This shift requires sales teams to demonstrate the real-world effectiveness and economic value of their products. Building strong evidence to support the value proposition of products is essential.

4. **Regulatory Changes**: Staying abreast of regulatory changes is crucial. New guidelines and policies can impact marketing practices and product positioning. Compliance with regulations such as GDPR (General Data Protection Regulation) is essential in maintaining trust and credibility.

The Path Forward

As Sarah reflected on her new role and the complexities of the pharmaceutical industry, she felt a mix of excitement and determination. She knew that her success as a sales manager would depend on her ability to lead her team with integrity, stay informed about industry trends, and build strong relationships with all stakeholders.

She also understood the importance of continuous learning and development. To be an effective leader, she would need to invest in her own growth as well as that of her team. This meant staying updated on industry developments, seeking out training opportunities, and fostering a culture of curiosity and innovation.

With her foundation in place, Sarah was ready to embark on this new chapter of her career. She was committed to making a positive impact, not only on her team but also on the healthcare providers and patients they served.

By grounding her journey in a solid understanding of the industry's landscape and her role within it, Sarah was ready to navigate the challenges and seize the opportunities that lay ahead as a pharmaceutical sales manager.

Chapter 2: Building Inclusive Leadership Skills

Embracing the Leadership Role

Sarah J. was settling into her new role as a pharmaceutical sales manager. The first few weeks were a whirlwind of meetings, onboarding sessions, and getting to know her team. She quickly realized that her success would depend not only on her industry knowledge but also on her ability to lead effectively. Leadership in the pharmaceutical industry, she discovered, was about more than just hitting sales targets. It was about building an inclusive, motivated, and high-performing team.

She remembered a conversation with her mentor, Paul, who had been a sales manager for over two decades. "Sarah," he had said, "the best leaders are those who understand that their team's success is their success. You have to cultivate an environment where everyone feels valued and included."

Understanding Inclusive Leadership

Inclusive leadership goes beyond traditional leadership styles by focusing on diversity, equity, and inclusion (DEI). It involves creating an environment where all team members feel respected, valued, and able to contribute their best work. Sarah knew this was crucial in a diverse industry like pharmaceuticals, where different perspectives could drive innovation and success.

Key Components of Inclusive Leadership:

1. **Awareness and Empathy:**
   - Recognizing and valuing the diverse backgrounds and experiences of team members.
   - Demonstrating empathy and understanding towards the unique challenges faced by individuals.

2. **Open Communication:**
   - Encouraging open dialogue and active listening.
   - Creating safe spaces where team members feel comfortable sharing their ideas and concerns.

3. **Fairness and Equity:**
   - Ensuring fair treatment and equal opportunities for all employees.

- Addressing biases and barriers that may hinder inclusivity.

4. **Collaboration and Participation:**
   - Promoting teamwork and collaboration.
   - Involving team members in decision-making processes and valuing their input.

The Power of Diversity

Sarah's team was a microcosm of diversity, representing different ages, genders, ethnicities, and professional backgrounds. She saw this diversity as a strength. Diverse teams bring a variety of perspectives, leading to more creative solutions and better decision-making. However, Sarah also knew that simply having a diverse team was not enough; she needed to foster

an inclusive culture where everyone felt they belonged.

She recalled a study by McKinsey & Company, which found that companies with diverse executive teams were more likely to outperform their peers in profitability. The study emphasized that diversity, when paired with an inclusive culture, leads to better financial performance and higher employee satisfaction.

Benefits of Diversity and Inclusion:

- **Enhanced Creativity and Innovation:** Different perspectives can lead to innovative solutions.
- **Improved Employee Engagement:** Inclusive workplaces foster a sense of belonging, leading to higher engagement and productivity.
- **Better Decision-Making:** Diverse teams are more likely to consider a wider range of options and make better decisions.

- **Attraction and Retention of Talent:** Inclusive companies attract top talent and retain employees by creating a supportive environment.

Implementing Inclusive Practices

To build an inclusive team, Sarah needed to implement practices that promoted diversity, equity, and inclusion. She began by assessing the current state of her team and identifying areas for improvement.

Steps to Foster an Inclusive Environment:

1. **Conduct a Diversity Audit:**
   - Assess the current diversity levels within the team.
   - Identify gaps and areas for improvement in representation.

2. **Develop DEI Training Programs:**
   - Provide training on unconscious bias, cultural competence, and inclusive practices.
   - Ensure that all team members understand the importance of DEI.

3. **Create Employee Resource Groups (ERGs):**
   - Establish ERGs to support underrepresented groups and foster a sense of community.
   - Encourage participation and provide resources to these groups.

4. **Implement Fair Hiring Practices:**
   - Standardize hiring processes to eliminate biases.
   - Use diverse interview panels and ensure equal opportunities for all candidates.

5. **Promote Open Communication:**
   - Encourage team members to share their experiences and ideas.
   - Create platforms for feedback and ensure that voices are heard and acted upon.

6. **Recognize and Celebrate Diversity:**
   - Acknowledge and celebrate cultural and individual differences.
   - Organize events and initiatives that highlight the diverse backgrounds of team members.

Leading by Example

Sarah knew that to build an inclusive team, she had to lead by example. Her actions and attitudes would set the tone for the rest of the team. She committed to being a visible advocate for diversity and inclusion, both in her words and actions.

Inclusive Leadership in Action:

1. **Demonstrating Empathy and Understanding:**
   - Sarah made a point of getting to know her team members personally. She took the time to understand their backgrounds, experiences, and challenges. This helped her build stronger relationships and foster trust.

2. **Encouraging Open Dialogue:**
   - In team meetings, Sarah encouraged open dialogue and active participation. She made sure that everyone had the opportunity to share their ideas and opinions. She also implemented anonymous feedback mechanisms to allow team members to express their thoughts without fear of repercussions.

3. **Addressing Biases:**
   - Sarah conducted regular training sessions on unconscious bias and cultural competence. She encouraged her team to reflect on their own biases and take steps to address them.

4. **Ensuring Fairness and Equity:**
   - Sarah reviewed the team's processes and policies to ensure they were fair and equitable. She worked to eliminate any barriers that might hinder inclusivity, such as biased performance reviews or unequal opportunities for advancement.

5. **Involving the Team in Decision-Making:**
   - Sarah involved her team in decision-making processes. She valued their input and made sure that their perspectives were considered. This not only led to better decisions but also increased team engagement and ownership.

Overcoming Challenges

Building an inclusive team wasn't without its challenges. Sarah faced resistance from some team members who were used to the old ways of working. She encountered biases and stereotypes that needed to be addressed. However, she remained committed to her goal and persevered.

She remembered a particular incident with one of her senior sales representatives, Tom. Tom was skeptical about the new focus on diversity and inclusion. He felt that it was just a corporate buzzword and didn't see its relevance to their work. Sarah decided to have a one-on-one conversation with him to address his concerns.

"Tom," she began, "I understand that you have reservations about our focus on diversity and inclusion. But I want to assure you that this is not just a buzzword. It's about creating an environment where everyone feels valued and can contribute their best work."

Tom listened as Sarah explained the benefits of diversity and inclusion, both for the team and the company. She shared examples of how diverse perspectives had led to innovative solutions and better decision-making. She also highlighted the positive impact on employee engagement and retention.

By the end of the conversation, Tom was more open to the idea. He agreed to participate in the upcoming DEI training and promised to keep an open mind. This conversation was a turning point for Sarah. It reinforced the importance of addressing concerns and involving team members in the journey towards inclusivity.

Continuous Improvement

Sarah knew that building an inclusive team was an ongoing process. It required continuous effort and commitment. She established regular check-ins and feedback sessions to monitor progress and make adjustments as needed.

Continuous Improvement Strategies:

1. **Regular Training and Development:**
   - Sarah scheduled regular DEI training sessions for her team. She also encouraged them to participate in external workshops and conferences to stay updated on best practices.

2. **Feedback Mechanisms:**
- She implemented regular feedback sessions to gather input from her team. This helped her identify areas for improvement and address any concerns promptly.

3. **Celebrating Successes:**
- Sarah celebrated the team's successes and milestones in their journey towards inclusivity. She recognized individual contributions and highlighted the positive impact on the team's performance.

4. **Adapting to Changes:**
- Sarah remained flexible and adaptable. She understood that the journey towards inclusivity was not linear and required adjustments along the way. She stayed open to new ideas and approaches.

The Path Ahead

As Sarah reflected on her progress, she felt a sense of accomplishment. She had made significant strides in building an inclusive team. Her efforts were reflected in the team's performance, engagement, and overall morale. The journey was far from over, but she was confident in her ability to lead her team towards a more inclusive future.

She realized that inclusive leadership was not just about implementing policies and practices. It was about embodying the values of diversity, equity, and inclusion in every aspect of her work. It was about being a role model for her team and creating a culture where everyone felt valued and empowered.

With a strong foundation in place, Sarah was ready to continue her journey as an inclusive leader. She was committed to fostering an environment where diversity thrived, and everyone had the opportunity to succeed.

Chapter 3: Effective Communication Strategies

Setting the Stage

Sarah J. had made significant strides in her new role as a pharmaceutical sales manager. She had laid a strong foundation by understanding the complexities of the pharmaceutical industry and committing to inclusive leadership practices. However, she quickly realized that effective communication was the linchpin that would hold everything together. Whether she was managing her team, interacting with healthcare providers, or collaborating with internal stakeholders, clear and open communication was essential.

The Importance of Communication in Sales Management

Effective communication in sales management goes beyond simply conveying information. It involves understanding the needs and perspectives of others, building trust, and fostering a collaborative environment. Sarah knew that her success as a leader depended on her ability to communicate effectively with her team and other stakeholders.

Key Aspects of Effective Communication:

1. **Clarity:** Ensuring that messages are clear and easily understood.
2. **Transparency:** Being open and honest in all communications.
3. **Empathy:** Understanding and addressing the emotions and concerns of others.
4. **Active Listening:** Fully engaging with others to understand their perspectives.
5. **Consistency:** Maintaining consistent messaging to avoid confusion and build trust.

Handling Difficult Conversations

One of the most challenging aspects of communication for any manager is handling difficult conversations. These could involve delivering critical feedback, addressing performance issues, or navigating conflicts within the team. Sarah knew that avoiding these conversations would only exacerbate problems and undermine her leadership.

Strategies for Handling Difficult Conversations:

1. **Prepare the Environment:**

- Choose a private, neutral location where the conversation can take place without interruptions.
- Ensure that both parties have enough time to discuss the issue thoroughly.

2. **Be Direct and Specific:**

- Clearly articulate the issue at hand and provide specific examples.
- Avoid vague language and ensure that your message is understood.

3. **Show Empathy and Respect:**
- Acknowledge the emotions and perspectives of the other person.
- Approach the conversation with empathy and a genuine desire to find a resolution.

4. **Stay Calm and Composed:**
- Manage your emotions and remain calm, even if the conversation becomes tense.
- Take a break if needed to avoid escalating the situation.

5. **Focus on Solutions:**
- Shift the focus from the problem to finding constructive solutions.
- Collaborate with the other person to develop a plan of action.

Fostering Open Communication

Sarah understood that fostering open communication within her team was essential for building trust and collaboration. She wanted her team members to feel comfortable sharing their ideas, concerns, and feedback.

Steps to Foster Open Communication:

1. **Create a Safe Environment:**

- Encourage team members to speak up without fear of judgment or repercussions.
- Ensure that all voices are heard and valued.

2. **Practice Active Listening:**
   - Give your full attention to the speaker and avoid interrupting.
   - Reflect on what is being said and ask clarifying questions.
3. **Provide Regular Feedback:**
   - Offer constructive feedback on a regular basis, both positive and negative.
   - Use feedback as an opportunity for growth and improvement.
4. **Encourage Collaboration:**
   - Promote teamwork and collaboration by facilitating open discussions and brainstorming sessions.
   - Recognize and celebrate team achievements.
5. **Be Transparent:**
   - Share relevant information with your team and keep them informed about important decisions and changes.
   - Address any concerns or rumors promptly to prevent misinformation.

Effective Communication with Healthcare Providers

As a sales manager in the pharmaceutical industry, Sarah's role involved not only managing her team but also building and maintaining relationships with healthcare providers (HCPs). Effective communication with HCPs was crucial for ensuring that they had the information and support they needed to make informed decisions about their patients' care.

Best Practices for Communicating with Healthcare Providers:

1. **Understand Their Needs:**
   - Take the time to understand the specific needs and challenges of each HCP.
   - Tailor your communication to address these needs and provide relevant solutions.
2. **Provide Valuable Information:**
   - Share up-to-date and accurate information about your products and their benefits.

- Highlight clinical data, case studies, and real-world evidence to support your claims.

3. **Be a Trusted Resource:**
   - Position yourself as a reliable and knowledgeable resource for HCPs.
   - Offer ongoing support and follow-up to address any questions or concerns.

4. **Build Long-Term Relationships:**
   - Focus on building long-term relationships rather than just making a sale.
   - Show genuine interest in the HCP's practice and patient outcomes.

5. **Use Multiple Channels:**
   - Utilize various communication channels, including face-to-face meetings, phone calls, emails, and digital platforms.
   - Ensure that your messaging is consistent across all channels.

Leveraging Technology for Effective Communication

In today's digital age, technology plays a crucial role in enhancing communication. Sarah recognized the importance of leveraging digital tools and platforms to improve communication with her team and external stakeholders.

Technology Tools for Enhanced Communication:

1. **Customer Relationship Management (CRM) Systems:**
   - Use CRM systems to manage and track interactions with HCPs.
   - Store and access important information about each HCP's preferences, needs, and history.
2. **Collaboration Platforms:**
   - Utilize collaboration platforms like Microsoft Teams, Slack, or Zoom to facilitate remote communication and teamwork.
   - Share documents, hold virtual meetings, and stay connected with your team.
3. **Email Marketing Tools:**
   - Use email marketing tools to send targeted and personalized messages to HCPs.
   - Track open rates, click-through rates, and responses to measure the effectiveness of your communication.
4. **Analytics and Reporting Tools:**
   - Use analytics tools to gather insights into communication patterns and effectiveness.
   - Generate reports to monitor progress and identify areas for improvement.

Building a Communication Strategy

To ensure effective communication within her team and with external stakeholders, Sarah decided to develop a comprehensive communication strategy. This strategy would serve as a roadmap for all communication activities and ensure consistency and alignment with the team's goals.

Components of a Communication Strategy:

1. **Objectives:**
   - Define the key objectives of your communication strategy. These could include improving team collaboration, enhancing relationships with HCPs, and increasing transparency.
2. **Audience:**
   - Identify the key audiences for your communication efforts. This could include team members, HCPs, internal stakeholders, and regulatory bodies.
3. **Key Messages:**

- Develop clear and consistent key messages that align with your objectives. Ensure that these messages are tailored to each audience.

4. **Channels:**
   - Determine the most effective communication channels for reaching each audience. This could include face-to-face meetings, emails, phone calls, virtual meetings, and social media.

5. **Timing:**
   - Establish a timeline for your communication activities. Determine the frequency and timing of updates, meetings, and other communication efforts.

6. **Feedback Mechanisms:**
   - Implement feedback mechanisms to gather input from your audience. This could include surveys, feedback forms, and regular check-ins.

7. **Evaluation:**
   - Regularly evaluate the effectiveness of your communication strategy. Use metrics and analytics to measure progress and identify areas for improvement.

Overcoming Communication Barriers

Despite her best efforts, Sarah knew that communication barriers could still arise. These could include misunderstandings, cultural differences, and resistance to change. She was determined to address these barriers proactively and ensure that communication remained effective.

Strategies for Overcoming Communication Barriers:

1. **Address Misunderstandings Promptly:**
   - Clarify any misunderstandings as soon as they arise. Use clear and concise language to avoid confusion.

2. **Be Culturally Sensitive:**
   - Recognize and respect cultural differences within your team and among HCPs. Adapt your communication style to be inclusive and respectful.

3. **Encourage Openness:**

- Foster an environment where team members feel comfortable expressing their concerns and providing feedback. Address any issues or resistance openly and constructively.

4. **Provide Training and Support:**
   - Offer training on effective communication skills, cultural competence, and conflict resolution. Provide ongoing support to help team members improve their communication abilities.

Conclusion

As Sarah reflected on the importance of effective communication, she realized that it was the glue that held everything together. From handling difficult conversations to fostering open communication and leveraging technology, effective communication was essential for building a high-performing and inclusive team.

With a clear communication strategy in place, Sarah was confident in her ability to lead her team to success. She knew that by prioritizing communication, she could build trust, enhance collaboration, and drive positive outcomes for her team and the healthcare providers they served.

Chapter 4: Advanced Sales Techniques and Strategies

A New Horizon for Sarah

Sarah J. was now well-versed in the fundamentals of pharmaceutical sales management. She had built a strong foundation in understanding the industry landscape, developing inclusive leadership skills, and mastering effective communication strategies. As she delved deeper into her role, she realized that to truly excel, she needed to refine her sales techniques and strategies. This chapter explores advanced sales techniques and strategies that can help sales managers in the pharmaceutical industry drive performance and achieve success.

Understanding Customer Needs

One of the first lessons Sarah learned was the importance of understanding customer needs. In the pharmaceutical industry, this means gaining a deep understanding of the healthcare providers (HCPs) she was engaging with. Each HCP had unique needs, preferences, and challenges, and tailoring her approach to meet these needs was crucial.

Steps to Understand Customer Needs:

1. **Conduct Research:**
   - Gather information about the HCPs, their practice, and their patient demographics.
   - Understand their specialties, interests, and any specific challenges they face.

2. **Ask Questions:**
   - Engage in meaningful conversations with HCPs to uncover their needs and concerns.
   - Use open-ended questions to encourage HCPs to share more about their practice and patient care.

3. **Listen Actively:**
   - Practice active listening to fully understand what the HCPs are saying.
   - Pay attention to both verbal and non-verbal cues to gauge their true needs and emotions.

4. **Analyze Data:**

- Utilize data analytics to identify trends and patterns in HCP behavior and preferences.
- Leverage insights from CRM systems to tailor your approach based on historical interactions.

Tailoring Sales Strategies

With a clear understanding of customer needs, Sarah was able to tailor her sales strategies to better serve HCPs. She knew that a one-size-fits-all approach would not work in the diverse and complex pharmaceutical industry. Instead, she focused on creating personalized and relevant strategies for each HCP.

Personalized Sales Strategies:

1. **Segmenting HCPs:**
   - Group HCPs based on their specialties, prescribing behaviors, and patient demographics.
   - Develop targeted strategies for each segment to address their specific needs.

2. **Customized Messaging:**
   - Tailor your messaging to highlight the benefits of your products relevant to each HCP's practice.
   - Use language and examples that resonate with the HCP's experiences and patient care goals.

3. **Flexible Approach:**
   - Be adaptable and willing to adjust your approach based on the HCP's feedback and changing needs.
   - Stay updated on the latest developments in their practice and adjust your strategy accordingly.

4. **Value Proposition:**
   - Clearly communicate the value proposition of your products, focusing on their benefits and outcomes.
   - Use evidence-based data, case studies, and real-world evidence to support your claims.

Leveraging Digital Tools and Technologies

In today's digital age, technology plays a pivotal role in enhancing sales effectiveness. Sarah recognized the importance of leveraging digital tools and platforms to reach HCPs more effectively and efficiently. By embracing digital transformation, she was able to streamline her sales processes and improve engagement with HCPs.

Key Digital Tools for Pharmaceutical Sales:
1. **Customer Relationship Management (CRM) Systems:**
   - Use CRM systems to manage and track interactions with HCPs.
   - Store and access important information about each HCP's preferences, needs, and history.
2. **Email Marketing Platforms:**
   - Utilize email marketing platforms to send targeted and personalized messages to HCPs.
   - Track open rates, click-through rates, and responses to measure the effectiveness of your communication.
3. **Virtual Meeting Tools:**
   - Conduct virtual meetings and webinars to engage with HCPs remotely.
   - Use video conferencing tools like Zoom or Microsoft Teams to facilitate face-to-face interactions.
4. **Data Analytics:**
   - Leverage data analytics to gather insights into HCP behavior and preferences.
   - Use predictive analytics to identify trends and forecast future needs.
5. **Social Media:**
   - Utilize social media platforms to connect with HCPs and share valuable content.
   - Participate in online forums and discussions to stay updated on industry trends and engage with the HCP community.

Building Long-Term Relationships

Sarah understood that building long-term relationships with HCPs was essential for sustained success. Rather than focusing solely on immediate sales, she aimed to build trust and establish herself as a reliable and knowledgeable resource for HCPs.

Strategies for Building Long-Term Relationships:
1. **Consistency and Reliability:**

- Be consistent in your communication and follow through on your commitments.
- Establish a reputation as a reliable partner who provides accurate and timely information.

2. **Educational Support:**
   - Provide educational resources and support to help HCPs stay informed about the latest developments in their field.
   - Offer access to webinars, conferences, and training sessions on relevant topics.

3. **Personalized Engagement:**
   - Tailor your interactions to each HCP's preferences and needs.
   - Send personalized messages and offers that are relevant to their practice and patient care goals.

4. **Regular Check-Ins:**
   - Schedule regular check-ins with HCPs to maintain the relationship and address any concerns.
   - Use these check-ins to gather feedback and identify opportunities for improvement.

5. **Value-Added Services:**
   - Offer value-added services that go beyond product sales, such as patient education materials or practice management tools.
   - Demonstrate your commitment to supporting HCPs in their overall practice, not just in product-related matters.

Implementing an Omnichannel Strategy

An omnichannel strategy involves providing a seamless and integrated customer experience across multiple channels. Sarah recognized that HCPs interacted with her company through various touchpoints, and ensuring a consistent and cohesive experience was crucial for building trust and loyalty.

Components of an Omnichannel Strategy:

1. **Integrated Communication Channels:**
   - Use a combination of face-to-face meetings, phone calls, emails, virtual meetings, and social media to engage with HCPs.

- Ensure that all channels are connected and provide a consistent message.

2. **Unified Customer Profile:**
   - Create a unified customer profile that consolidates information from all interaction channels.
   - Use this profile to personalize interactions and provide relevant information.

3. **Seamless Experience:**
   - Ensure that HCPs have a seamless experience when interacting with your company across different channels.
   - Provide consistent messaging, branding, and support regardless of the channel used.

4. **Data-Driven Insights:**
   - Use data from all channels to gain a comprehensive understanding of HCP behavior and preferences.
   - Leverage these insights to refine your strategies and improve engagement.

5. **Responsive and Agile Approach:**
   - Be responsive to HCP needs and adapt quickly to changing circumstances.
   - Use feedback and data to make real-time adjustments to your strategy.

Utilizing Key Performance Indicators (KPIs)

To measure the effectiveness of her sales strategies, Sarah needed to implement key performance indicators (KPIs). These metrics would help her track progress, identify areas for improvement, and make data-driven decisions.

Essential KPIs for Pharmaceutical Sales:

1. **Sales Revenue:**
   - Track total sales revenue and revenue growth over time.
   - Analyze revenue by product, region, and customer segment.

2. **Market Share:**
   - Monitor your company's market share relative to competitors.

- Identify trends and changes in market share over time.
3. **Customer Acquisition:**
    - Measure the number of new HCPs acquired and their contribution to sales.
    - Track the effectiveness of acquisition campaigns and strategies.
4. **Customer Retention:**
    - Monitor customer retention rates and identify reasons for attrition.
    - Implement strategies to improve retention and build long-term loyalty.
5. **Customer Satisfaction:**
    - Use surveys and feedback forms to measure HCP satisfaction with your products and services.
    - Analyze feedback to identify areas for improvement and enhance the customer experience.
6. **Sales Cycle Length:**
    - Track the average length of the sales cycle from initial contact to closing the sale.
    - Identify bottlenecks and streamline processes to reduce the sales cycle length.
7. **Conversion Rates:**
    - Measure the percentage of leads that convert into sales.
    - Analyze conversion rates by channel and strategy to identify the most effective approaches.

Continuous Learning and Development

Sarah knew that the pharmaceutical industry was constantly evolving, and staying updated on the latest developments was essential for maintaining a competitive edge. She committed to continuous learning and development for herself and her team.

Strategies for Continuous Learning and Development:

1. **Ongoing Training:**
    - Provide regular training sessions on new products, industry trends, and advanced sales techniques.
    - Encourage team members to participate in external workshops and conferences.
2. **Mentorship and Coaching:**

- Establish a mentorship program to provide guidance and support to team members.
- Offer coaching sessions to help team members develop their skills and achieve their goals.

3. **Knowledge Sharing:**
   - Foster a culture of knowledge sharing within the team.
   - Encourage team members to share their experiences, insights, and best practices.

4. **Access to Resources:**
   - Provide access to industry publications, research papers, and online courses.
   - Encourage team members to stay informed about the latest developments in their field.

5. **Feedback and Improvement:**
   - Implement regular feedback sessions to gather input from team members and HCPs.
   - Use feedback to identify areas for improvement and make necessary adjustments.

Case Studies and Success Stories

Sarah found that sharing case studies and success stories was a powerful way to illustrate the effectiveness of advanced sales techniques and strategies. These real-world examples provided valuable insights and inspiration for her team.

Case Study 1: Personalized Engagement with HCPs

Background: A pharmaceutical company launched a new diabetes medication and needed to engage with endocrinologists and general practitioners.

Approach: The sales team conducted in-depth research to understand the specific needs and preferences of each HCP. They segmented the HCPs based on their specialties and patient demographics. The team developed personalized messaging and tailored their approach for each segment. They used a combination of face-to-face meetings, virtual webinars, and email marketing to engage with the HCPs.

Outcome: The personalized approach resulted in higher engagement rates and increased product adoption. The company achieved a 30% increase in sales within the first six months of the launch. HCPs appreciated the tailored messaging and relevant information, leading to stronger relationships and long-term loyalty.

Case Study 2: Leveraging Digital Tools for Enhanced Communication

Background: A pharmaceutical company needed to improve communication and engagement with HCPs in rural areas.

Approach: The sales team implemented a CRM system to manage and track interactions with HCPs. They used virtual meeting tools to conduct webinars and online training sessions. The team also utilized email marketing platforms to send targeted and personalized messages. Data analytics was used to gather insights and refine the communication strategy.

Outcome: The use of digital tools significantly improved communication and engagement with HCPs in rural areas. The company saw a 25% increase in webinar attendance and a 20% increase in email open rates. The CRM system helped streamline processes and provided valuable insights into HCP preferences and behavior.

Case Study 3: Building Long-Term Relationships with Educational Support

Background: A pharmaceutical company wanted to strengthen relationships with oncologists and hematologists.

Approach: The sales team focused on providing educational support and resources to HCPs. They organized webinars, conferences, and training sessions on the latest developments in oncology and hematology. The team also provided access to research papers, case studies, and patient education materials.

Outcome: The educational support approach led to stronger relationships and increased trust with HCPs. The company achieved a

40% increase in product adoption and a 35% increase in customer retention. HCPs valued the ongoing support and educational resources, which enhanced their practice and patient care.

Conclusion

As Sarah J. continued her journey as a pharmaceutical sales manager, she realized that mastering advanced sales techniques and strategies was essential for achieving success. By understanding customer needs, tailoring sales strategies, leveraging digital tools, building long-term relationships, implementing an omnichannel strategy, utilizing KPIs, and committing to continuous learning, she was able to drive performance and achieve her goals.

The journey was challenging, but with a clear focus on excellence and a commitment to her team and customers, Sarah was confident in her ability to lead her team to success. The insights and experiences she gained along the way not only enhanced her own skills but also empowered her team to reach new heights.

With a solid foundation in place, Sarah was ready to navigate the ever-evolving pharmaceutical industry and make a lasting impact on the healthcare providers and patients she served.

Chapter 5: Performance Metrics and KPIs

The Importance of Metrics

Sarah J. had come a long way since stepping into her role as a pharmaceutical sales manager. She had laid a solid foundation in understanding the industry, building inclusive leadership skills, mastering communication strategies, and refining her sales techniques. Now, she faced the crucial task of measuring her team's performance to ensure they were on the right track. This chapter delves into the importance of performance metrics and key performance indicators (KPIs) in pharmaceutical sales management, offering detailed guidance on how to implement and utilize them effectively.

Understanding Performance Metrics and KPIs

Performance metrics and KPIs are essential tools that help managers measure progress, identify areas for improvement, and make data-driven decisions. In the pharmaceutical industry, where precision and compliance are critical, these metrics provide valuable insights into the effectiveness of sales strategies and overall business performance.

Key Definitions:

- **Performance Metrics:** Quantitative measures used to gauge the efficiency and effectiveness of various processes and activities.
- **Key Performance Indicators (KPIs):** Specific, measurable values that indicate how well an organization is achieving its key business objectives. Sarah knew that implementing the right metrics and KPIs would allow her to track her team's performance accurately and align their efforts with the company's strategic goals.

Selecting the Right KPIs

Choosing the right KPIs is crucial for effectively measuring performance. Sarah needed to identify KPIs that were relevant, actionable, and aligned with her team's objectives. She focused on a balanced mix of financial, operational, and customer-centric KPIs to provide a comprehensive view of performance.

Criteria for Selecting KPIs:

1. **Relevance:** KPIs should be directly related to the team's goals and objectives.
2. **Measurability:** KPIs should be quantifiable and based on reliable data.
3. **Actionability:** KPIs should provide insights that lead to actionable steps.
4. **Timeliness:** KPIs should be tracked regularly to provide up-to-date information.
5. **Alignment:** KPIs should align with the company's overall strategy and objectives.

Example KPIs for Pharmaceutical Sales:

1. **Sales Revenue:**
   - Total sales revenue generated by the team.
   - Revenue growth over time.
2. **Market Share:**
   - Percentage of market share relative to competitors.
   - Trends and changes in market share.
3. **Customer Acquisition:**
   - Number of new healthcare providers (HCPs) acquired.
   - Contribution of new HCPs to total sales.
4. **Customer Retention:**
   - Customer retention rates and reasons for attrition.
   - Strategies to improve retention and build loyalty.
5. **Customer Satisfaction:**
   - Survey scores and feedback from HCPs.
   - Areas for improvement based on feedback.
6. **Sales Cycle Length:**
   - Average length of the sales cycle from initial contact to closing the sale.
   - Strategies to streamline the sales process.
7. **Conversion Rates:**

- Percentage of leads that convert into sales.
- Analysis of conversion rates by channel and strategy.

8. **Product Adoption Rates:**
   - Rates of adoption for new products.
   - Factors influencing adoption and strategies to improve uptake.

9. **Training and Development:**
   - Participation rates in training programs.
   - Improvement in skills and knowledge post-training.

10. **Compliance and Ethics:**
    - Adherence to regulatory requirements and ethical standards.
    - Incidents of non-compliance and corrective actions.

Implementing KPIs

Once Sarah had selected the relevant KPIs, the next step was to implement them effectively. This involved setting clear targets, establishing a system for tracking and reporting, and ensuring that her team understood the importance of these metrics.

Steps to Implement KPIs:

1. **Set Clear Targets:**
   - Define specific, measurable targets for each KPI.
   - Ensure that targets are challenging yet achievable.

2. **Establish Tracking Systems:**
   - Implement systems to track and report KPIs regularly.
   - Use CRM systems, data analytics tools, and dashboards for real-time tracking.

3. **Communicate with the Team:**
   - Ensure that the team understands the KPIs and their importance.
   - Regularly communicate progress and provide updates.

4. **Review and Adjust:**
   - Regularly review KPI performance and identify areas for improvement.
   - Adjust strategies and targets as needed based on performance data.

Utilizing Data Analytics

In the digital age, data analytics plays a critical role in measuring and improving performance. Sarah recognized the importance of leveraging data analytics to gain deeper insights into her team's performance and make informed decisions.

Benefits of Data Analytics:

1. **Informed Decision-Making:**
   - Use data-driven insights to make strategic decisions.
   - Identify trends, patterns, and areas for improvement.

2. **Predictive Analytics:**
   - Use predictive analytics to forecast future trends and performance.
   - Anticipate challenges and opportunities.

3. **Personalized Engagement:**
   - Analyze customer data to tailor engagement strategies.
   - Provide personalized solutions based on customer needs and preferences.

4. **Performance Tracking:**
   - Monitor real-time performance and adjust strategies accordingly.
   - Use dashboards and reports to visualize KPI performance.

Implementing Data Analytics:

1. **Data Collection:**
   - Collect data from various sources, including CRM systems, sales reports, and customer feedback.
   - Ensure data accuracy and reliability.

2. **Data Analysis:**
   - Use data analytics tools to analyze and interpret data.
   - Identify key insights and trends.

3. **Reporting:**
   - Create regular reports and dashboards to track KPI performance.
   - Share insights with the team and senior management.

4. **Continuous Improvement:**
   - Use data insights to drive continuous improvement.

- Implement changes based on data analysis and track their impact.

Enhancing Sales Strategies

With a solid understanding of performance metrics and data analytics, Sarah was ready to enhance her sales strategies. She focused on optimizing her team's efforts to maximize performance and achieve their targets.

Advanced Sales Strategies:

1. **Account-Based Selling:**
   - Focus on high-value accounts and tailor strategies to meet their specific needs.
   - Build strong relationships with key decision-makers.
2. **Solution Selling:**
   - Position products as solutions to specific customer problems.
   - Highlight the value and benefits of the products.
3. **Cross-Selling and Upselling:**
   - Identify opportunities to sell additional products or upgrade existing ones.
   - Use data insights to identify potential cross-selling and upselling opportunities.
4. **Customer-Centric Approach:**
   - Put the customer at the center of all sales activities.
   - Focus on understanding and meeting customer needs.
5. **Sales Enablement:**
   - Provide the team with the tools, resources, and training they need to succeed.
   - Use technology to streamline sales processes and improve efficiency.

Implementing Enhanced Sales Strategies:

1. **Develop a Sales Playbook:**
   - Create a comprehensive sales playbook that outlines best practices, strategies, and processes.
   - Include detailed information on customer personas, sales scripts, and objection handling.
2. **Training and Development:**

- Provide ongoing training and development opportunities for the team.
- Focus on enhancing skills in areas such as solution selling, negotiation, and relationship-building.

3. **Sales Coaching:**
   - Implement regular coaching sessions to provide guidance and support.
   - Use data insights to identify areas for improvement and tailor coaching accordingly.

4. **Collaboration and Teamwork:**
   - Foster a collaborative environment where team members can share insights and best practices.
   - Encourage teamwork and peer support.

5. **Technology and Tools:**
   - Leverage technology and tools to enhance sales processes.
   - Use CRM systems, data analytics tools, and sales enablement platforms to support the team.

Monitoring and Adjusting Strategies

Sarah knew that continuous monitoring and adjustment of strategies were essential for sustained success. By regularly reviewing performance data and gathering feedback, she could identify areas for improvement and make necessary adjustments.

Monitoring and Adjusting Strategies:

1. **Regular Performance Reviews:**
   - Conduct regular performance reviews to assess progress and identify areas for improvement.
   - Use KPI data to guide discussions and set new targets.

2. **Feedback Mechanisms:**
   - Implement feedback mechanisms to gather input from the team and customers.
   - Use feedback to identify pain points and areas for improvement.

3. **Agile Approach:**

- Adopt an agile approach to sales strategy, allowing for flexibility and quick adjustments.
- Use data insights to make real-time adjustments and optimize performance.

4. **Continuous Improvement:**
   - Foster a culture of continuous improvement within the team.
   - Encourage team members to identify opportunities for improvement and share their ideas.

5. **Celebrate Successes:**
   - Recognize and celebrate the team's successes and achievements.
   - Use positive reinforcement to motivate and inspire the team.

Case Studies and Success Stories

To illustrate the effectiveness of performance metrics and KPIs, Sarah shared case studies and success stories with her team. These real-world examples provided valuable insights and inspiration.

Case Study 1: Improving Sales Revenue with Data-Driven Insights

Background: A pharmaceutical company needed to improve sales revenue for a new oncology medication.

Approach: The sales team implemented data analytics to gain insights into HCP behavior and preferences. They used CRM systems to track interactions and identify high-value accounts. The team developed personalized engagement strategies based on data insights.

Outcome: The data-driven approach resulted in a 35% increase in sales revenue within six months. The team was able to identify and target high-value accounts effectively, leading to higher conversion rates and increased product adoption.

Case Study 2: Enhancing Customer Satisfaction through Personalized Engagement

Background: A pharmaceutical company wanted to improve customer satisfaction and build long-term relationships with HCPs.

Approach: The sales team focused on personalized engagement strategies, using data insights to tailor their approach. They implemented regular check-ins, provided educational support, and offered value-added services.

Outcome: Customer satisfaction scores improved by 40%, and customer retention rates increased by 30%. HCPs appreciated the personalized engagement and ongoing support, leading to stronger relationships and long-term loyalty.

Case Study 3: Streamlining Sales Processes with Technology

Background: A pharmaceutical company needed to streamline sales processes and improve efficiency.

Approach: The sales team implemented CRM systems, data analytics tools, and sales enablement platforms. They used these tools to track performance, analyze data, and streamline processes.

Outcome: Sales cycle length was reduced by 25%, and conversion rates increased by 20%. The use of technology improved efficiency and provided valuable insights into performance, leading to better decision-making and optimized sales strategies.

Conclusion

As Sarah J. continued her journey as a pharmaceutical sales manager, she realized the critical importance of performance metrics and KPIs in driving success. By selecting the right KPIs, implementing data analytics, enhancing sales strategies, and continuously monitoring and adjusting her approach, she was able to lead her team to new heights.

The journey was challenging, but with a clear focus on excellence and a commitment to her team and customers, Sarah was confident in her ability to achieve commercial excellence in the pharmaceutical industry. The insights and experiences she gained along the way not only enhanced her own skills but also empowered her team to reach new heights.

With a solid foundation in place, Sarah was ready to navigate the ever-evolving pharmaceutical industry and make a lasting impact on the healthcare providers and patients she served.

Chapter 6: Navigating the Challenges of Pharmaceutical Sales

Introduction

Sarah J. had achieved significant milestones as a pharmaceutical sales manager. She had built a strong foundation in understanding the industry, inclusive leadership, effective communication, advanced sales strategies, and performance metrics. However, the pharmaceutical sales landscape is fraught with challenges that require constant vigilance and adaptability. This chapter explores the various challenges faced by pharmaceutical sales managers and provides strategies to navigate them effectively.

The Complexity of the Pharmaceutical Industry

The pharmaceutical industry is one of the most regulated and complex industries in the world. Sales managers must navigate a labyrinth of regulations, compliance requirements, and market dynamics. Sarah quickly realized that staying compliant and adaptable was crucial for success.

Key Challenges in the Pharmaceutical Industry:

1. **Regulatory Compliance:**
   - Adhering to stringent regulations set by agencies such as the FDA, EMA, and other global regulatory bodies.
   - Ensuring that marketing and sales practices comply with legal and ethical standards.
2. **Market Dynamics:**

- Navigating a highly competitive market with numerous players, including established pharmaceutical companies and biotech startups.
- Adapting to changes in market conditions, such as pricing pressures and patent expirations.

3. **Innovation and R&D:**
    - Keeping up with rapid advancements in medical research and technology.
    - Ensuring that sales teams are well-informed about new products and scientific developments.

4. **Healthcare Provider (HCP) Relationships:**
    - Building and maintaining strong relationships with HCPs while navigating their busy schedules and varying preferences.
    - Addressing the diverse needs of different HCPs, from general practitioners to specialists.

Strategies for Navigating Regulatory Compliance

Sarah understood that regulatory compliance was non-negotiable. She needed to ensure that her team adhered to all regulations while effectively promoting their products. She implemented several strategies to navigate this complex landscape.

Ensuring Compliance:

1. **Regular Training:**
    - Provide ongoing training on regulatory requirements and compliance best practices.
    - Ensure that all team members are up-to-date with the latest regulations and guidelines.

2. **Clear Policies and Procedures:**
    - Develop clear policies and procedures for all sales and marketing activities.
    - Ensure that these policies are communicated effectively and consistently enforced.

3. **Internal Audits:**
    - Conduct regular internal audits to ensure compliance with regulations.

- Identify and address any potential compliance issues promptly.

4. **Ethical Standards:**
   - Promote a culture of integrity and ethical behavior.
   - Encourage team members to report any unethical practices or compliance concerns.

Example Compliance Training Program:

Module	Description
Introduction to Compliance	Overview of regulatory bodies and their roles.
Key Regulations	Detailed review of key regulations (e.g., FDA, EMA).
Ethical Sales Practices	Guidelines for ethical behavior and interactions with HCPs.
Reporting and Documentation	Best practices for documenting and reporting sales activities.
Case Studies	Real-world examples of compliance challenges and how to address them.

Adapting to Market Dynamics

The pharmaceutical market is constantly evolving, with new competitors, changing pricing pressures, and shifting customer preferences. Sarah knew that staying ahead required agility and a deep understanding of market dynamics.

Adapting to Market Changes:

1. **Market Research:**
   - Conduct regular market research to stay informed about industry trends, competitor activities, and customer preferences.
   - Use data analytics to gain insights into market dynamics and identify opportunities and threats.

2. **Agile Strategies:**

- Develop agile strategies that can be quickly adapted to changing market conditions.
- Encourage a culture of flexibility and innovation within the team.

3. **Competitive Analysis:**
   - Conduct thorough competitive analysis to understand the strengths and weaknesses of competitors.
   - Identify areas where your products can offer a unique value proposition.

4. **Customer Feedback:**
   - Gather and analyze feedback from HCPs to understand their evolving needs and preferences.
   - Use this feedback to refine your sales strategies and product offerings.

Example Market Research Report:

Section	Description
Industry Trends	Overview of key industry trends and developments.
Competitor Analysis	Analysis of key competitors and their market positioning.
Customer Insights	Summary of customer feedback and preferences.
Market Opportunities	Identification of potential opportunities for growth.
Threats and Challenges	Analysis of potential threats and challenges.

Leveraging Innovation and R&D

Innovation and R&D are at the heart of the pharmaceutical industry. Sales managers must stay informed about new products and scientific developments to effectively communicate their value to HCPs.

Staying Informed and Educated:

1. **Continuous Learning:**
   - Encourage continuous learning and professional development within the team.

- Provide access to resources such as scientific journals, webinars, and conferences.

2. **Collaboration with R&D:**
   - Foster collaboration between the sales and R&D teams.
   - Ensure that sales teams are well-informed about new products, clinical trial results, and scientific advancements.

3. **Product Training:**
   - Develop comprehensive training programs for new products.
   - Ensure that sales representatives have a deep understanding of the science behind the products and their clinical benefits.

4. **Customer Education:**
   - Provide educational resources to HCPs to help them stay informed about new treatments and advancements.
   - Organize educational events such as webinars, conferences, and workshops.

Example Product Training Program:

Module	Description
Product Overview	Introduction to the new product, including its indications and benefits.
Clinical Data	Review of clinical trial results and scientific evidence.
Mechanism of Action	Detailed explanation of the product's mechanism of action.
Competitive Positioning	Comparison with existing treatments and competitors.
Sales Strategies	Best practices for effectively promoting the product to HCPs.

Building Strong HCP Relationships

Building and maintaining strong relationships with HCPs is crucial for success in pharmaceutical sales. Sarah focused on creating meaningful connections and providing value to HCPs.

Strategies for Building Strong HCP Relationships:

1. **Personalized Engagement:**

- Tailor your approach to meet the unique needs and preferences of each HCP.
- Use data insights to personalize interactions and provide relevant information.

2. **Educational Support:**
   - Offer educational resources and support to help HCPs stay informed and improve patient care.
   - Provide access to clinical data, case studies, and patient education materials.

3. **Consistent Communication:**
   - Maintain regular and consistent communication with HCPs.
   - Use a variety of communication channels, including face-to-face meetings, virtual meetings, and emails.

4. **Value-Added Services:**
   - Offer value-added services that go beyond product promotion, such as practice management tools and patient support programs.
   - Demonstrate your commitment to supporting HCPs in their overall practice.

5. **Trust and Transparency:**
   - Build trust by being transparent and honest in all interactions.
   - Ensure that your communication is clear, accurate, and free from bias.

Example HCP Engagement Plan:

Action	Description
Personalized Emails	Send personalized emails with relevant product information and updates.
Educational Webinars	Organize webinars on clinical topics and new product developments.
Regular Check-Ins	Schedule regular check-ins to gather feedback and address any concerns.
Value-Added Resources	Provide access to practice management tools and patient education materials.

| Trust-Building Activities | Conduct transparent and honest discussions about product benefits and limitations. |

Managing and Motivating the Sales Team

One of the biggest challenges Sarah faced was managing and motivating her sales team. She needed to ensure that her team remained engaged, motivated, and aligned with the company's goals.

Strategies for Managing and Motivating the Sales Team:

1. **Clear Goals and Expectations:**
   - Set clear and achievable goals for the team.
   - Ensure that each team member understands their role and responsibilities.

2. **Regular Feedback and Recognition:**
   - Provide regular feedback on performance and recognize achievements.
   - Celebrate successes and milestones to boost morale and motivation.

3. **Professional Development:**
   - Offer opportunities for professional development and career growth.
   - Provide training and resources to help team members improve their skills and knowledge.

4. **Team Collaboration:**
   - Foster a collaborative and supportive team environment.
   - Encourage teamwork and peer support.

5. **Incentives and Rewards:**
   - Implement incentive programs to reward high performance.
   - Offer both financial and non-financial rewards to motivate the team.

Example Incentive Program:

Incentive	Description
Performance Bonuses	Financial bonuses for achieving or exceeding sales targets.
Recognition Awards	Awards for outstanding performance, such as "Sales Representative of the Month."
Professional Development	Opportunities for advanced training and professional development.
Team Outings	Team-building activities and outings to celebrate successes.
Career Advancement	Opportunities for career advancement and promotions.

Overcoming Resistance and Managing Change

Change is inevitable in the pharmaceutical industry, whether it's due to new regulations, market dynamics, or internal restructuring. Sarah needed to effectively manage change and overcome resistance within her team.

Strategies for Managing Change:

1. **Communication:**
   - Communicate changes clearly and transparently.
   - Explain the reasons for the change and how it will benefit the team and organization.
2. **Involvement:**
   - Involve the team in the change process and seek their input.
   - Encourage team members to share their concerns and suggestions.
3. **Support:**
   - Provide support and resources to help the team navigate the change.
   - Offer training and guidance to ensure a smooth transition.
4. **Flexibility:**
   - Be flexible and open to feedback during the change process.

- Make adjustments as needed based on the team's input and feedback.

5. **Positive Reinforcement:**
   - Use positive reinforcement to motivate the team and build confidence.
   - Celebrate small wins and progress during the change process.

Example Change Management Plan:

Step	Description
Communication Plan	Develop a communication plan to announce the change and explain its benefits.
Team Meetings	Hold team meetings to discuss the change and gather feedback.
Training Sessions	Provide training sessions to help the team adapt to the change.
Support Resources	Offer support resources, such as guides and FAQs, to assist the team.
Progress Check-Ins	Schedule regular check-ins to monitor progress and address any issues.

Leveraging Technology for Sales Success

Technology plays a crucial role in enhancing sales effectiveness and efficiency. Sarah recognized the importance of leveraging technology to support her team and drive success.

Key Technologies for Pharmaceutical Sales:

1. **Customer Relationship Management (CRM) Systems:**
   - Use CRM systems to manage and track interactions with HCPs.
   - Store and access important information about each HCP's preferences, needs, and history.

2. **Data Analytics Tools:**
   - Leverage data analytics tools to gain insights into HCP behavior and preferences.
   - Use predictive analytics to identify trends and forecast future needs.

3. **Virtual Meeting Platforms:**
   - Conduct virtual meetings and webinars to engage with HCPs remotely.

- Use video conferencing tools like Zoom or Microsoft Teams to facilitate face-to-face interactions.

4. **Sales Enablement Platforms:**
   - Use sales enablement platforms to provide the team with the tools, resources, and training they need to succeed.
   - Streamline sales processes and improve efficiency.

5. **Mobile Applications:**
   - Utilize mobile applications to provide real-time access to information and resources.
   - Enable sales representatives to stay connected and productive while on the go.

Example Technology Implementation Plan:

Technology	Description
CRM System	Implement a CRM system to manage and track HCP interactions.
Data Analytics Tools	Use data analytics tools to gain insights and make data-driven decisions.
Virtual Meeting Platforms	Conduct virtual meetings and webinars to engage with HCPs remotely.
Sales Enablement Platforms	Provide the team with tools, resources, and training to support their efforts.
Mobile Applications	Enable real-time access to information and resources through mobile apps.

Conclusion

Navigating the challenges of pharmaceutical sales requires a combination of strategic planning, adaptability, and continuous improvement. Sarah J. understood that staying compliant, adaptable, and informed was crucial for success. By implementing effective strategies for regulatory compliance, market adaptation, innovation, HCP relationships, team management, change management, and technology utilization, she was able to lead her team through the complexities of the pharmaceutical industry.

The journey was challenging, but with a clear focus on excellence and a commitment to her team and customers, Sarah was confident in her ability to achieve commercial excellence. The insights and experiences she gained along the way not only enhanced her own skills but also empowered her team to reach new heights.

With a solid foundation in place, Sarah was ready to navigate the ever-evolving pharmaceutical industry and make a lasting impact on the healthcare providers and patients she served.

Chapter 7: Cultivating a High-Performance Sales Culture

Introduction

Sarah J. had successfully navigated the complexities of the pharmaceutical industry, built an inclusive and effective team, and implemented advanced sales strategies and performance metrics. Yet, she knew that sustaining long-term success required more than just good practices and strategies—it demanded a high-performance culture. This chapter explores how Sarah cultivated a high-performance sales culture that fostered continuous improvement, innovation, and engagement, ensuring her team not only met but exceeded their goals.

The Essence of a High-Performance Culture

A high-performance culture is characterized by a shared commitment to excellence, accountability, and continuous improvement. It creates an environment where employees are motivated, engaged, and empowered to perform at their best. Sarah understood that building such a culture required a combination of clear vision, strong leadership, effective communication, and supportive systems.

Key Elements of a High-Performance Culture:

1. **Clear Vision and Values:**
   - A shared understanding of the organization's mission, vision, and values.
   - Alignment of individual and team goals with the organization's strategic objectives.

2. **Leadership Commitment:**
   - Leaders who model the desired behaviors and set high standards.
   - Consistent support and recognition from leadership.

3. **Employee Engagement:**
   - A sense of ownership and accountability among employees.
   - Opportunities for growth, development, and contribution.

4. **Continuous Improvement:**

- A focus on learning, innovation, and agility.
- Systems and processes that support ongoing improvement.

5. **Recognition and Rewards:**
    - Regular recognition of achievements and contributions.
    - Incentive programs that reward high performance and innovation.

Setting a Clear Vision and Values

Sarah began by clearly articulating the vision and values of her team. She wanted her team to understand not just what they were doing, but why they were doing it. This alignment was crucial for fostering a sense of purpose and direction.

Steps to Define Vision and Values:

1. **Engage the Team:**
    - Involve the team in discussions about the organization's mission, vision, and values.
    - Encourage input and feedback to ensure buy-in and alignment.

2. **Articulate the Vision:**
    - Clearly define the long-term vision and goals of the team.
    - Ensure that the vision is inspiring, realistic, and aligned with the organization's strategic objectives.

3. **Define Core Values:**
    - Identify the core values that will guide the team's behaviors and decisions.
    - Ensure that these values are aligned with the organization's culture and goals.

4. **Communicate Consistently:**
    - Regularly communicate the vision and values to the team.
    - Reinforce these messages through meetings, communications, and actions.

Example Vision and Values Statement:

Vision	To be the most trusted and innovative pharmaceutical sales team, delivering exceptional value to healthcare providers and improving patient outcomes.
Core Values	**Integrity:** We act with honesty and integrity in all our interactions.
	Excellence: We strive for excellence in everything we do.
	Collaboration: We work together to achieve common goals.
	Innovation: We embrace change and seek innovative solutions.
	Customer-Centricity: We put our customers at the center of everything we do.

Demonstrating Leadership Commitment

Leadership commitment is crucial for building and sustaining a high-performance culture. Sarah knew that her actions and behaviors would set the tone for the rest of the team. She focused on modeling the desired behaviors and providing consistent support and recognition.

Strategies for Demonstrating Leadership Commitment:

1. **Lead by Example:**
   - Model the behaviors and attitudes you expect from your team.
   - Demonstrate a commitment to the team's vision and values in your actions.

2. **Provide Support:**
   - Offer regular support and guidance to team members.
   - Be available to address concerns, provide feedback, and help with challenges.

3. **Recognize and Celebrate:**
   - Regularly recognize and celebrate team and individual achievements.
   - Use recognition to reinforce desired behaviors and achievements.

4. **Communicate Openly:**
   - Maintain open and transparent communication with the team.

- Share updates, progress, and challenges honestly and promptly.
5. **Encourage Feedback:**
   - Encourage team members to provide feedback and suggestions.
   - Act on feedback to demonstrate that their input is valued and considered.

Example Leadership Actions:

Action	Description
Regular Team Meetings	Hold regular team meetings to discuss progress, challenges, and goals.
One-on-One Check-Ins	Conduct regular one-on-one check-ins with team members to provide support and gather feedback.
Recognition Programs	Implement recognition programs to celebrate achievements and contributions.
Transparent Communication	Share regular updates on team performance, organizational changes, and strategic goals.
Feedback Mechanisms	Create mechanisms for team members to provide feedback and suggestions, such as surveys and suggestion boxes.

Fostering Employee Engagement

Employee engagement is the emotional commitment that employees have to their organization and its goals. Engaged employees are motivated, productive, and more likely to stay with the organization. Sarah focused on creating an environment where her team felt valued, supported, and motivated.

Strategies for Fostering Employee Engagement:
1. **Provide Growth Opportunities:**
   - Offer opportunities for professional development and career advancement.
   - Support continuous learning through training, workshops, and conferences.
2. **Encourage Autonomy:**
   - Empower team members to take ownership of their work and make decisions.

- Provide autonomy while offering guidance and support as needed.
3. **Build Strong Relationships:**
   - Foster a sense of camaraderie and teamwork within the team.
   - Encourage collaboration and support among team members.
4. **Promote Work-Life Balance:**
   - Encourage a healthy work-life balance to prevent burnout.
   - Offer flexible working arrangements and support for personal well-being.
5. **Solicit and Act on Feedback:**
   - Regularly gather feedback from team members about their experiences and needs.
   - Act on feedback to address concerns and improve the work environment.

Example Employee Engagement Plan:

Initiative	Description
Professional Development Program	Offer a structured professional development program with training, workshops, and mentorship opportunities.
Empowerment Initiatives	Implement initiatives to empower team members, such as decision-making authority and ownership of projects.
Team Building Activities	Organize regular team-building activities to strengthen relationships and foster collaboration.
Wellness Programs	Provide wellness programs that support physical and mental well-being, such as fitness classes and counseling.
Feedback Systems	Establish feedback systems, such as regular surveys and suggestion boxes, to gather and act on team input.

Embracing Continuous Improvement

Continuous improvement is the ongoing effort to enhance processes, products, and services. In a high-performance culture, continuous improvement is embedded in the organization's DNA. Sarah encouraged her team to adopt a mindset of constant learning and innovation.

Strategies for Embracing Continuous Improvement:

1. **Encourage Innovation:**
   - Foster a culture where innovation is encouraged and valued.
   - Provide time and resources for creative thinking and experimentation.

2. **Implement Lean Practices:**
   - Adopt lean practices to streamline processes and eliminate waste.
   - Use tools such as Kaizen and Six Sigma to drive continuous improvement.

3. **Promote Learning and Development:**
   - Encourage team members to pursue continuous learning and development.
   - Offer access to educational resources, courses, and certifications.

4. **Conduct Regular Reviews:**
   - Conduct regular reviews of processes and performance to identify areas for improvement.
   - Use data and feedback to drive decision-making and improvements.

5. **Celebrate Small Wins:**
   - Recognize and celebrate small wins and incremental improvements.
   - Use these successes to build momentum and motivation for further improvements.

Example Continuous Improvement Plan:

Initiative	Description
Innovation Workshops	Conduct regular innovation workshops to brainstorm new ideas and solutions.

Lean Process Reviews	Implement lean process reviews to identify inefficiencies and areas for improvement.
Learning and Development Programs	Offer ongoing learning and development programs to enhance skills and knowledge.
Performance Reviews	Conduct regular performance reviews to assess progress and identify improvement opportunities.
Celebrating Successes	Celebrate small wins and incremental improvements to build momentum and motivation.

Implementing Recognition and Rewards

Recognition and rewards are powerful tools for motivating employees and reinforcing desired behaviors. Sarah knew that a well-designed recognition and rewards program would help sustain a high-performance culture.

Strategies for Recognition and Rewards:

1. **Regular Recognition:**
   - Provide regular recognition for achievements and contributions.
   - Use various forms of recognition, such as verbal praise, written acknowledgments, and public recognition.

2. **Incentive Programs:**
   - Implement incentive programs that reward high performance and innovation.
   - Offer both financial and non-financial rewards, such as bonuses, gift cards, and extra time off.

3. **Personalized Rewards:**
   - Tailor rewards to individual preferences and needs.
   - Use personalized rewards to show appreciation and value for each team member.

4. **Peer Recognition:**
   - Encourage peer recognition to build a supportive and collaborative team environment.

- Implement peer recognition programs, such as "Employee of the Month" and "Peer Appreciation Awards."

5. **Celebrate Milestones:**
   - Celebrate important milestones and achievements, such as hitting sales targets or completing major projects.
   - Use celebrations to reinforce the team's commitment to excellence and success.

Example Recognition and Rewards Program:

Recognition Method	Description
Verbal Praise	Provide verbal praise and acknowledgment during team meetings and one-on-one check-ins.
Written Acknowledgments	Send written acknowledgments, such as thank-you notes and emails, to recognize achievements.
Public Recognition	Recognize achievements publicly through newsletters, bulletin boards, and company announcements.
Financial Incentives	Offer financial incentives, such as bonuses and gift cards, for high performance and innovation.
Personalized Rewards	Provide personalized rewards, such as extra time off or customized gifts, to show appreciation.
Peer Recognition Programs	Implement peer recognition programs, such as "Employee of the Month" and "Peer Appreciation Awards."
Celebration Events	Organize celebration events, such as team lunches and parties, to celebrate milestones and achievements.

Case Studies and Success Stories

To illustrate the effectiveness of a high-performance culture, Sarah shared case studies and success stories with her team. These real-world examples provided valuable insights and inspiration.

Case Study 1: Achieving Excellence through Clear Vision and Values

Background: A pharmaceutical sales team needed to improve performance and alignment with organizational goals.

Approach: The team engaged in discussions to define their vision and core values. They articulated a clear vision and set of values that aligned with the organization's strategic objectives. The vision and values were communicated consistently and reinforced through leadership actions.

Outcome: The team experienced increased alignment and motivation. Sales performance improved by 25%, and employee engagement scores rose significantly. The clear vision and values provided a sense of purpose and direction, driving the team to achieve excellence.

Case Study 2: Enhancing Engagement through Professional Development

Background: A pharmaceutical sales team faced challenges with employee engagement and retention.

Approach: The team implemented a structured professional development program that offered training, workshops, and mentorship opportunities. Team members were encouraged to pursue continuous learning and career advancement.

Outcome: Employee engagement scores improved by 30%, and retention rates increased by 20%. Team members felt valued and supported, leading to higher motivation and productivity. The professional development program contributed to a high-performance culture and long-term success.

Case Study 3: Driving Continuous Improvement through Innovation

Background: A pharmaceutical sales team needed to enhance efficiency and innovation.

Approach: The team adopted lean practices and conducted regular innovation workshops. They implemented process reviews to identify inefficiencies and areas for improvement. Team members were encouraged to experiment with new ideas and solutions.

Outcome: Process efficiency improved by 35%, and innovation scores increased significantly. The team identified and implemented several innovative solutions that enhanced performance and customer satisfaction. The focus on continuous improvement and innovation fostered a high-performance culture.

Case Study 4: Motivating Team Members through Recognition and Rewards

Background: A pharmaceutical sales team wanted to enhance motivation and recognition for achievements.

Approach: The team implemented a comprehensive recognition and rewards program that included regular recognition, incentive programs, personalized rewards, and peer recognition. Achievements and milestones were celebrated through various events and acknowledgments.

Outcome: Motivation and morale improved significantly, leading to a 20% increase in sales performance. Team members felt appreciated and valued, which reinforced their commitment to excellence. The recognition and rewards program contributed to a supportive and high-performance culture.

Conclusion

Cultivating a high-performance sales culture requires a combination of clear vision, strong leadership, employee engagement, continuous improvement, and effective recognition and rewards. Sarah J. understood that building and sustaining such a culture was crucial for long-term success in the pharmaceutical industry.

By defining a clear vision and values, demonstrating leadership commitment, fostering employee engagement, embracing continuous improvement, and implementing recognition and rewards, Sarah was able to create an environment where her team thrived. The insights and experiences she gained along the way not only enhanced her own leadership skills but also empowered her team to achieve excellence. The journey was challenging, but with a clear focus on excellence and a commitment to her team and customers, Sarah was confident in her ability to lead her team to new heights. With a solid foundation in place, she was ready to navigate the ever-evolving pharmaceutical industry and make a lasting impact on the healthcare providers and patients she served.

Chapter 8: Leveraging Technology and Innovation in Pharmaceutical Sales

Introduction

Sarah J. had cultivated a high-performance culture within her pharmaceutical sales team, focusing on vision, values, leadership, engagement, continuous improvement, and recognition. As she continued to drive her team towards excellence, she recognized the crucial role of technology and innovation in sustaining their success. This chapter explores how Sarah navigated and leveraged technology to enhance her team's performance, streamline processes, and create value for healthcare providers (HCPs) and patients.

The Role of Technology in Pharmaceutical Sales

In the fast-paced and highly regulated pharmaceutical industry, technology plays a pivotal role in enabling sales teams to achieve their goals. From customer relationship management (CRM) systems to data analytics tools, technology provides the infrastructure and capabilities needed to enhance efficiency, improve communication, and drive informed decision-making.

Implementing CRM Systems

One of the first steps Sarah took was to implement a robust CRM system. She understood that having a centralized platform for managing customer interactions was essential for maintaining organization and efficiency. After evaluating several options, Sarah decided to implement Salesforce CRM.

Benefits of CRM Systems:

1. **Centralized Data Management:**
   - Salesforce allowed Sarah's team to store and organize customer data in one place, making it easy to access and update information about HCPs, interactions, and sales activities.
   - The CRM provided a comprehensive view of each HCP, including past interactions, preferences, and notes, which helped the sales team personalize their approach.
2. **Enhanced Communication:**

- Salesforce enabled the team to schedule and track follow-ups with HCPs, ensuring that no opportunities were missed.
- Automated reminders and notifications helped the team stay on top of tasks and appointments.

3. **Data-Driven Insights:**
   - The CRM's reporting and analytics features allowed Sarah to analyze customer data and gain insights into behavior and preferences.
   - By identifying trends and opportunities, Sarah could make more informed decisions about sales strategies and resource allocation.

4. **Improved Collaboration:**
   - Salesforce facilitated collaboration among team members by allowing them to share information and updates in real-time.
   - The CRM's Chatter feature enabled team members to communicate and collaborate on customer interactions and sales opportunities.

Example of CRM Implementation:

Sarah conducted a needs assessment to identify the specific requirements of her sales team. She then selected Salesforce CRM for its comprehensive features and user-friendly interface. The customization process involved configuring fields, templates, and automation rules to align with the team's workflows. Training sessions were held to ensure that all team members were comfortable using the CRM. Regular monitoring and feedback sessions were conducted to optimize the system's use.

Step	Description
Needs Assessment	Identify specific needs and requirements for the CRM system.
Platform Selection	Choose Salesforce CRM for its comprehensive features and user-friendly interface.
Customization	Configure fields, templates, and automation rules to align with workflows.

| Training | Provide comprehensive training to ensure team members are comfortable using the system. |
| Monitoring | Regularly monitor usage and gather feedback for continuous improvement. |

Leveraging Data Analytics and Business Intelligence

Sarah knew that data-driven decision-making was crucial for optimizing performance and staying competitive. She implemented Tableau, a data analytics and business intelligence tool, to gain deeper insights into sales performance, customer behavior, and market trends.

Benefits of Data Analytics:

1. **Informed Decision-Making:**
   - Tableau allowed Sarah to use data-driven insights to make strategic decisions, such as identifying high-potential opportunities and allocating resources effectively.
   - The tool provided visualizations that made it easy to interpret complex data.

2. **Predictive Analytics:**
   - By using predictive analytics, Sarah's team could forecast future sales and customer behavior, enabling them to anticipate challenges and opportunities.
   - This helped in proactive planning and strategy development.

3. **Performance Tracking:**
   - Tableau's dashboards allowed Sarah to monitor real-time performance and track key performance indicators (KPIs).
   - She could visualize data in various formats, making it easier to identify trends and areas for improvement.

4. **Personalized Engagement:**
   - Data insights enabled Sarah's team to tailor their engagement strategies to individual HCPs, providing personalized solutions based on customer needs and preferences.

Example of Data Analytics Implementation:

Sarah began by collecting data from various sources, including Salesforce CRM, sales reports, and customer feedback. She used Tableau to analyze and interpret the data, creating visualizations that highlighted key insights. Regular reports and dashboards were created to track performance and share insights with the team. Based on the data analysis, Sarah implemented changes to improve sales strategies and monitor their impact.

Step	Description
Data Collection	Collect data from Salesforce CRM, sales reports, and customer feedback.
Data Analysis	Use Tableau to analyze and interpret data, creating visualizations for insights.
Reporting	Create regular reports and dashboards to track performance and share insights.
Continuous Improvement	Use data insights to drive improvements and track their impact.

Embracing Virtual Meeting Platforms

With the rise of digital communication, Sarah embraced Zoom as a virtual meeting platform to enhance engagement with HCPs. This allowed her team to conduct remote meetings, webinars, and product demonstrations, overcoming geographical barriers and reaching a wider audience.

Benefits of Virtual Meeting Platforms:

1. **Remote Engagement:**
   - Zoom enabled Sarah's team to conduct meetings and presentations with HCPs remotely, overcoming geographical barriers and reaching a wider audience.

- The platform's ease of use and reliability made it a popular choice among HCPs.

2. **Flexibility:**
    - The team could schedule meetings and webinars at convenient times for HCPs and offer on-demand access to recorded sessions.
    - This flexibility was appreciated by busy HCPs who could access the content at their convenience.

3. **Cost-Effectiveness:**
    - By reducing travel and accommodation costs, Zoom allowed Sarah's team to allocate resources more efficiently.

    - The savings could be reinvested in other areas, such as training and development.

4. **Enhanced Interaction:**
    - Zoom's interactive features, such as Q&A sessions, polls, and breakout rooms, allowed the team to engage participants and gather feedback in real-time.
    - This interactive approach made the sessions more engaging and valuable for HCPs.

Example of Virtual Meeting Implementation:

Sarah selected Zoom for its user-friendly interface and robust features. She provided training to the team on how to use Zoom effectively for meetings and webinars. The team scheduled virtual meetings and webinars at convenient times for HCPs, promoting the sessions through email and social media. During the sessions, interactive features were used to engage participants and gather feedback. Recorded sessions were made available on-demand, and follow-up communications were sent to address any outstanding questions.

Step	Description

Platform Selection	Choose Zoom for its user-friendly interface and robust features.
Training	Provide training on how to use Zoom effectively for meetings and webinars.
Scheduling and Promotion	Schedule meetings and webinars and promote them through email and social media.
Engagement	Use interactive features to engage participants and gather feedback.
Follow-Up	Provide access to recorded sessions and follow up with participants.

Enhancing Sales Enablement

Sales enablement involves providing sales representatives with the tools, resources, and training they need to succeed. Sarah implemented Highspot, a comprehensive sales enablement platform, to support her team in their interactions with HCPs.

Benefits of Sales Enablement:

1. **Improved Efficiency:**
   - Highspot streamlined sales processes and reduced administrative tasks, allowing sales representatives to focus on engaging with HCPs.
   - The platform provided easy access to relevant resources and information.

2. **Enhanced Training:**
   - Highspot offered training modules and resources to improve the team's skills and knowledge.
   - Continuous learning and development were supported through regular updates and new content.

3. **Consistent Messaging:**
   - The platform ensured consistent messaging and branding across all interactions with HCPs.
   - Sales scripts and templates supported communication and ensured alignment with marketing strategies.

4. **Data-Driven Insights:**
   - Highspot provided data insights that helped tailor engagement strategies and improve performance.

- The team could track and analyze sales activities and outcomes to identify best practices and areas for improvement.

Example of Sales Enablement Implementation:
Sarah conducted a needs assessment to identify the specific requirements of her sales team. She selected Highspot for its comprehensive features and ease of use. The platform was customized to align with the team's processes and workflows. Training sessions were held to ensure that all team members were comfortable using Highspot. Regular monitoring and feedback sessions were conducted to optimize the platform's use and ensure continuous improvement.

Step	Description
Needs Assessment	Identify specific needs and challenges of the sales team.
Platform Selection	Choose Highspot for its comprehensive features and ease of use.
Customization	Customize the platform to align with processes and workflows.
Training	Provide training on how to use the platform effectively.
Monitoring	Regularly monitor usage and gather feedback for continuous improvement.

Utilizing Mobile Applications
In today's mobile-driven world, having access to information and resources on the go is essential. Sarah implemented Veeva CRM Mobile, a mobile application that ensured her sales team could stay connected and productive while in the field.

Benefits of Mobile Applications:
1. **Real-Time Access:**
   - Veeva CRM Mobile provided real-time access to information and resources while on the go.
   - Sales representatives could access customer data, product information, and sales materials from their mobile devices.
2. **Enhanced Communication:**

67

- The app allowed team members to communicate with each other and with HCPs through mobile messaging and email.
- Updates, resources, and feedback could be shared instantly.

3. **Task Management:**
   - Veeva CRM Mobile enabled sales representatives to manage tasks and schedules, using reminders and notifications to stay on top of activities.
   - This improved organization and efficiency.

4. **Data Capture:**
   - The app allowed for capturing customer interactions and feedback directly, ensuring accurate and timely data entry.
   - This data could be synced with the central CRM system for comprehensive tracking and analysis.

Example of Mobile Application Implementation:

Sarah selected Veeva CRM Mobile for its robust features and integration with Salesforce CRM. The app was customized to align with the team's workflows and processes. Training sessions were held to ensure that all team members were comfortable using Veeva CRM Mobile. Regular monitoring and feedback sessions were conducted to optimize the app's use and ensure continuous improvement.

Step	Description
Platform Selection	Choose Veeva CRM Mobile for its robust features and integration with Salesforce CRM.
Customization	Customize the app to align with workflows and processes.
Training	Provide training on how to use the app effectively.
Integration	Integrate the app with Salesforce CRM for seamless data flow.
Monitoring	Regularly monitor usage and gather feedback for continuous improvement.

Embracing Digital Marketing Tools

Sarah recognized the power of digital marketing in reaching and engaging HCPs and patients. She implemented HubSpot, a digital marketing platform, to create personalized and effective marketing campaigns.

Benefits of Digital Marketing Tools:

1. **Targeted Campaigns:**
   - HubSpot allowed Sarah's team to create personalized marketing campaigns based on customer data and preferences.
   - The platform enabled targeted engagement with the right audience.

2. **Multi-Channel Engagement:**
   - HubSpot supported engagement through multiple channels, such as email, social media, and content marketing.
   - This ensured consistent messaging across all channels.

3. **Analytics and Insights:**
   - The platform provided analytics tools to track and analyze the performance of marketing campaigns.
   - Data insights were used to optimize strategies and improve results.

4. **Automation:**
   - HubSpot's automation features enabled the team to automate repetitive tasks, such as email campaigns and social media posts.
   - This saved time and increased efficiency.

Example of Digital Marketing Implementation:

Sarah selected HubSpot for its comprehensive features and ease of use. She developed a digital marketing plan that outlined goals, target audience, and strategies. High-quality content was created in various formats, such as blog posts, videos, and infographics. The team executed digital marketing campaigns and used analytics tools to track performance. Data insights were used to optimize strategies and improve results continuously.

Step	Description
Platform Selection	Choose HubSpot for its comprehensive features and ease of use.

Campaign Planning	Develop a comprehensive digital marketing plan with goals, target audience, and strategies.
Content Creation	Develop high-quality content in various formats.
Execution and Monitoring	Execute campaigns and monitor performance using analytics tools.
Optimization	Use data insights to optimize strategies and improve results.

Case Studies and Success Stories

To illustrate the impact of leveraging technology and innovation, Sarah shared case studies and success stories with her team. These real-world examples provided valuable insights and inspiration.

Case Study 1: Enhancing Customer Relationships with Salesforce CRM

Background: Sarah's team needed to improve organization and efficiency in managing customer interactions.

Approach: The team implemented Salesforce CRM to centralize customer data, track interactions, and automate follow-ups. They customized the system to align with their processes and provided comprehensive training to team members.

Outcome: Customer interactions became more organized and efficient. The team was able to track and manage follow-ups effectively, leading to a 30% increase in customer satisfaction and a 25% improvement in sales performance.

Case Study 2: Driving Sales with Tableau Analytics

Background: Sarah's team wanted to optimize their performance and identify new opportunities.

Approach: The team implemented Tableau to analyze sales data, customer behavior, and market trends. They used predictive analytics to forecast future sales and identify high-potential opportunities.

Outcome: The team gained valuable insights that informed their strategies and decision-making. Sales performance improved by 20%, and the team identified several new opportunities that contributed to revenue growth.

Case Study 3: Expanding Reach with Zoom

Background: Sarah's team needed to overcome geographical barriers and engage with a wider audience.

Approach: The team implemented Zoom to conduct remote meetings, webinars, and product demonstrations. They scheduled sessions at convenient times for HCPs and used interactive features to engage participants.

Outcome: The team was able to reach a wider audience and conduct more meetings and presentations. Engagement and feedback from HCPs improved, leading to a 35% increase in meeting attendance and a 15% increase in sales.

Case Study 4: Streamlining Processes with Highspot

Background: Sarah's team needed to improve efficiency and support their sales representatives.

Approach: The team implemented Highspot to provide resources, training, and tools to sales representatives. They organized content libraries, developed training modules, and provided ongoing support.

Outcome: Sales representatives became more efficient and effective in their interactions with HCPs. Sales performance improved by 25%, and the team reported higher satisfaction and confidence in their roles.

Case Study 5: Engaging Customers with HubSpot

Background: Sarah's team wanted to enhance their digital marketing efforts and reach more HCPs and patients.

Approach: The team implemented HubSpot to create personalized and targeted campaigns. They developed high-quality content, scheduled campaigns, and used analytics tools to track performance.

Outcome: The team achieved higher engagement rates and improved the effectiveness of their marketing campaigns. Website traffic increased by 40%, and lead generation improved by 30%.

Conclusion

Leveraging technology and embracing innovation are crucial for sustaining success in the pharmaceutical industry. Sarah J. understood the importance of implementing CRM systems, data analytics, virtual meeting platforms, sales enablement tools, mobile applications, and digital marketing strategies to enhance her team's performance and create value for HCPs and patients.

By implementing these technologies and fostering a culture of continuous improvement and innovation, Sarah was able to drive significant improvements in efficiency, engagement, and sales performance. The insights and experiences she gained along the way not only enhanced her own leadership skills but also empowered her team to reach new heights.

The journey was challenging, but with a clear focus on leveraging technology and innovation, Sarah was confident in her ability to lead her team to new levels of excellence. With a solid foundation in place, she was ready to navigate the ever-evolving pharmaceutical industry and make a lasting impact on the healthcare providers and patients she served.

Chapter 9: Building and Sustaining Customer Relationships

Introduction

Having established a high-performance culture, leveraged technology, and embraced innovation, Sarah J. knew that the next critical step was to focus on building and sustaining strong customer relationships. In the pharmaceutical industry, relationships with healthcare providers (HCPs) are fundamental to success. This chapter explores how Sarah and her team developed strategies and practices to foster trust, engagement, and loyalty among their HCP customers, ultimately driving better outcomes for both the company and the patients they serve.

Understanding Customer Needs

One of the first principles Sarah emphasized to her team was the importance of understanding the unique needs and preferences of their HCP customers. This required a combination of listening, data analysis, and personalized engagement.

Steps to Understand Customer Needs:

1. **Active Listening:**
   - Encourage sales representatives to listen actively during interactions with HCPs.
   - Train them to ask open-ended questions and pay attention to both verbal and non-verbal cues.

2. **Data Analysis:**
   - Use CRM systems like Salesforce to gather and analyze data on HCP preferences, behaviors, and feedback.
   - Identify patterns and trends that can inform personalized engagement strategies.

3. **Feedback Mechanisms:**
   - Implement regular surveys and feedback forms to gather insights directly from HCPs.
   - Use this feedback to continuously improve products, services, and engagement tactics.

Example of Understanding Customer Needs:

Sarah's team used Salesforce CRM to track interactions with HCPs and record detailed notes about their preferences and concerns. They also conducted quarterly surveys to gather additional insights. This combination of qualitative and quantitative data helped the team tailor their approach to meet the specific needs of each HCP.

Step	Description
Active Listening	Encourage listening during interactions and asking open-ended questions.
Data Analysis	Use CRM systems to gather and analyze data on HCP preferences and behaviors.
Feedback Mechanisms	Implement surveys and feedback forms to gather insights directly from HCPs.

Building Trust and Credibility

Building trust and credibility with HCPs is essential for establishing long-term relationships. Sarah focused on ensuring that her team acted with integrity, transparency, and reliability in all their interactions.

Strategies for Building Trust:

1. **Consistency:**
   - Ensure that the team provides consistent and reliable information.
   - Follow through on commitments and promises.
2. **Transparency:**
   - Be transparent about product information, including benefits, risks, and limitations.
   - Share relevant updates and changes promptly.
3. **Expertise:**
   - Position the team as knowledgeable experts in their field.
   - Provide valuable insights and information that help HCPs make informed decisions.
4. **Empathy:**
   - Show genuine empathy and understanding for the challenges and needs of HCPs.
   - Build rapport by showing that the team cares about their success and the well-being of their patients.

Example of Building Trust and Credibility:

Sarah ensured that her team received continuous training to stay updated on the latest product information and industry trends. They were encouraged to be transparent and honest in all communications, even when discussing challenges or limitations. By consistently delivering on their promises and providing valuable expertise, the team built strong trust and credibility with their HCP customers.

Strategy	Description
Consistency	Provide consistent and reliable information, and follow through on commitments.
Transparency	Be transparent about product information and share relevant updates promptly.
Expertise	Position the team as knowledgeable experts and provide valuable insights.
Empathy	Show genuine empathy and understanding for HCP challenges and needs.

Personalizing Engagement

Personalized engagement is key to building strong relationships with HCPs. Sarah's team used the data and insights gathered from their CRM system and feedback mechanisms to tailor their interactions and provide a more personalized experience.

Techniques for Personalizing Engagement:

1. **Segmenting Customers:**
   - Use data to segment HCPs based on their specialties, preferences, and behaviors.
   - Develop tailored engagement strategies for each segment.
2. **Customized Communications:**
   - Personalize emails, calls, and meetings based on the specific interests and needs of each HCP.
   - Use CRM data to reference past interactions and provide relevant updates.
3. **Value-Added Services:**
   - Offer additional resources and support that align with the HCP's needs, such as educational materials, training sessions, and patient support programs.
   - Provide customized solutions that address specific challenges faced by HCPs.

4. **Proactive Follow-Up:**
    - Follow up proactively after meetings and interactions to address any questions or concerns.
    - Use reminders and notifications in the CRM system to ensure timely follow-ups.

Example of Personalizing Engagement:

Sarah's team segmented their HCP customers into different categories based on their specialties and preferences. For example, oncologists received tailored information about oncology products and related research, while cardiologists received updates on cardiovascular products. Customized emails and follow-up calls referenced previous interactions and provided relevant content. This personalized approach resulted in higher engagement and satisfaction among HCPs.

Technique	Description
Segmenting Customers	Use data to segment HCPs based on specialties, preferences, and behaviors.
Customized Communications	Personalize emails, calls, and meetings based on HCP interests and needs.
Value-Added Services	Offer additional resources and support that align with HCP needs.
Proactive Follow-Up	Follow up proactively to address questions and concerns, using CRM reminders.

Leveraging Technology for Better Engagement

Technology played a crucial role in helping Sarah's team enhance their engagement with HCPs. By leveraging tools such as Salesforce, Zoom, Highspot, Veeva CRM Mobile, and HubSpot, the team was able to provide a seamless and integrated experience for their customers.

Benefits of Leveraging Technology:

1. **Efficiency:**
    - Technology streamlined processes and reduced administrative tasks, allowing the team to focus more on customer interactions.
    - Automated reminders and workflows ensured that nothing fell through the cracks.
2. **Real-Time Data:**
    - Access to real-time data allowed the team to stay updated on customer interactions and preferences.

- Real-time insights enabled more timely and relevant engagement.

3. **Integrated Experience:**
   - Integration between different tools ensured that data and insights were seamlessly shared across platforms.
   - This provided a cohesive and consistent experience for HCPs.

4. **Enhanced Communication:**
   - Virtual meeting platforms like Zoom facilitated remote engagement and allowed for more frequent interactions.
   - Mobile applications like Veeva CRM Mobile ensured that the team could stay connected and productive while in the field.

Example of Leveraging Technology:

Sarah's team used Salesforce to manage customer data and track interactions, Zoom for virtual meetings and webinars, Highspot for sales enablement and training, Veeva CRM Mobile for real-time access to information, and HubSpot for digital marketing campaigns. The integration of these tools provided a seamless and efficient experience for both the team and their HCP customers.

Benefit	Description
Efficiency	Streamlined processes and reduced administrative tasks, allowing focus on interactions.
Real-Time Data	Access to real-time data for timely and relevant engagement.
Integrated Experience	Seamless sharing of data and insights across platforms for a cohesive experience.
Enhanced Communication	Virtual meetings and mobile access for frequent and productive interactions.

Providing Continuous Value

To sustain strong customer relationships, Sarah emphasized the importance of continuously providing value to HCPs. This involved staying attuned to their evolving needs and offering solutions that addressed their challenges.

Strategies for Providing Continuous Value:

1. **Educational Support:**
   - Offer ongoing education and training through webinars, workshops, and online courses.
   - Provide access to the latest research, clinical guidelines, and best practices.

2. **Resource Provision:**
   - Develop and distribute high-quality educational materials, such as brochures, whitepapers, and videos.
   - Create patient support programs and resources to help HCPs better manage patient care.

3. **Collaborative Partnerships:**
   - Foster collaborative partnerships with HCPs by involving them in research, clinical trials, and advisory boards.
   - Encourage feedback and collaboration to co-create solutions that meet their needs.

4. **Proactive Problem-Solving:**
   - Anticipate potential challenges and proactively offer solutions and support.
   - Stay engaged and responsive to address issues as they arise.

Example of Providing Continuous Value:

Sarah's team organized regular webinars and workshops on various medical topics, providing HCPs with valuable education and training. They also developed a library of educational materials and patient support resources. By involving HCPs in research and clinical trials, the team fostered collaborative partnerships. This continuous value provision reinforced the team's commitment to supporting HCPs and their patients.

Strategy	Description
Educational Support	Offer ongoing education and training through webinars, workshops, and online courses.
Resource Provision	Develop and distribute high-quality educational materials and patient support programs.

Collaborative Partnerships	Foster collaborative partnerships through research and advisory boards.
Proactive Problem-Solving	Anticipate challenges and offer proactive solutions and support.

Measuring and Evaluating Relationship Success

To ensure the effectiveness of their relationship-building efforts, Sarah implemented metrics and evaluation methods to measure success. This allowed the team to identify areas for improvement and make data-driven decisions.

Key Metrics for Measuring Relationship Success:

1. **Customer Satisfaction:**
   - Use surveys and feedback forms to measure HCP satisfaction with interactions and support.
   - Track satisfaction scores and identify areas for improvement.

2. **Engagement Levels:**
   - Monitor engagement metrics, such as attendance at webinars, response rates to emails, and participation in surveys.
   - Use CRM data to track the frequency and quality of interactions.

3. **Retention Rates:**
   - Measure the retention rates of HCP customers over time.
   - Identify factors that contribute to retention and areas that need attention.

4. **Net Promoter Score (NPS):**
   - Use NPS surveys to gauge the likelihood of HCPs recommending the company to their peers.
   - Analyze NPS results to understand overall sentiment and loyalty.

Example of Measuring and Evaluating Relationship Success:

Sarah's team conducted quarterly surveys to measure customer satisfaction and gather feedback. They used CRM data to track engagement levels and retention rates. NPS surveys were also conducted to assess customer loyalty. The team regularly reviewed these metrics and used the insights to refine their strategies and improve their relationship-building efforts.

Metric	Description
Customer Satisfaction	Use surveys and feedback forms to measure satisfaction and identify areas for improvement.
Engagement Levels	Monitor engagement metrics and track frequency and quality of interactions.
Retention Rates	Measure retention rates of HCP customers and identify factors that contribute to retention.
Net Promoter Score (NPS)	Use NPS surveys to gauge likelihood of HCPs recommending the company.

Conclusion

Building and sustaining strong customer relationships is fundamental to success in the pharmaceutical industry. Sarah J. understood the importance of understanding customer needs, building trust and credibility, personalizing engagement, leveraging technology, providing continuous value, and measuring relationship success.

By implementing these strategies and practices, Sarah's team was able to foster trust, engagement, and loyalty among their HCP customers. The insights and experiences gained along the way not only enhanced their relationship-building skills but also contributed to better outcomes for both the company and the patients they served.

With a solid foundation in place, Sarah and her team were well-equipped to navigate the complexities of the pharmaceutical industry and continue making a lasting impact on the healthcare providers and patients they served.

Chapter 10: Ethical Considerations and Compliance

Introduction

As Sarah J. continued to drive her pharmaceutical sales team towards excellence, she recognized that maintaining ethical standards and ensuring compliance with industry regulations were paramount. The pharmaceutical industry is highly regulated, and adherence to ethical practices is crucial for building trust and credibility with healthcare providers (HCPs) and customers. This chapter explores the importance of understanding industry regulations, ensuring ethical practices in sales activities, and building trust and credibility, building on the previous chapters.

Understanding Industry Regulations and Compliance Requirements

The pharmaceutical industry operates under stringent regulations designed to protect patient safety and ensure the efficacy of medical products. Understanding and adhering to these regulations is essential for any sales team.

Key Areas of Compliance:

1. **Regulatory Bodies:**
   - Familiarize with key regulatory bodies such as the Food and Drug Administration (FDA) in the United States, the European Medicines Agency (EMA) in Europe, and other national regulatory agencies.
   - Understand the specific guidelines and regulations these bodies enforce, which govern the marketing, sales, and distribution of pharmaceutical products.

2. **Good Promotional Practices:**
   - Ensure all promotional activities comply with guidelines set by regulatory bodies, such as the FDA's Office of Prescription Drug Promotion (OPDP) and EMA's regulations on pharmaceutical marketing.

- Avoid misleading claims, ensure that all information provided is accurate and balanced, and disclose all relevant safety information.

3. **Anti-Kickback and Bribery Laws:**
   - Adhere to laws such as the Anti-Kickback Statute in the US and the Bribery Act in the UK, which prohibit offering, paying, soliciting, or receiving any form of remuneration to induce or reward the referral of business.
   - Implement policies and training programs to prevent any activities that could be construed as kickbacks or bribery.

4. **Data Privacy Regulations:**
   - Comply with data privacy regulations such as the General Data Protection Regulation (GDPR) in Europe and the Health Insurance Portability and Accountability Act (HIPAA) in the US.
   - Ensure that all patient and HCP data is handled securely and confidentially, with appropriate consent obtained for its use.

Example of Compliance Implementation:

Sarah organized comprehensive training sessions for her team to ensure they were well-versed in relevant regulations. She also implemented a compliance monitoring system to track promotional activities and ensure adherence to guidelines. Regular audits and reviews were conducted to identify and address any compliance issues promptly.

Area	Description
Regulatory Bodies	Understand guidelines from FDA, EMA, and other agencies.
Good Promotional Practices	Ensure promotional activities are accurate and balanced.
Anti-Kickback and Bribery Laws	Adhere to laws preventing remuneration for business referrals.
Data Privacy Regulations	Comply with GDPR, HIPAA, and other data privacy laws.

Ensuring Ethical Practices in Sales Activities

Ethical practices are foundational to maintaining integrity and trust in the pharmaceutical industry. Sarah emphasized the importance of ethical behavior in all sales activities.

Key Elements of Ethical Sales Practices:

1. **Transparency:**
   - Ensure that all interactions with HCPs and customers are transparent. Provide clear and accurate information about products, including potential side effects and limitations.
   - Avoid any actions that could be perceived as deceptive or manipulative.

2. **Respect for HCPs and Patients:**
   - Treat HCPs and patients with respect and consideration. Understand their needs and priorities, and avoid pressuring them into decisions.
   - Prioritize patient well-being in all sales strategies and decisions.

3. **Conflict of Interest Management:**
   - Identify and manage any potential conflicts of interest. Ensure that personal or financial interests do not influence professional decisions and actions.
   - Implement policies to disclose and address conflicts of interest transparently.

4. **Fair Competition:**
   - Engage in fair competition by respecting competitors and avoiding disparaging remarks or unethical tactics.
   - Focus on highlighting the strengths and benefits of your own products rather than undermining competitors.

5. **Continuous Training and Development:**
   - Provide ongoing training on ethical practices and industry regulations. Ensure that the team is aware of the latest guidelines and best practices.
   - Foster a culture of continuous improvement and ethical behavior.

Example of Ethical Practice Implementation:

Sarah introduced an ethics training program that covered key principles and real-world scenarios. She also created an ethics hotline where team members could report concerns anonymously. Regular discussions on ethical dilemmas and best practices were held to reinforce the importance of ethical behavior.

Element	Description
Transparency	Provide clear and accurate information about products.
Respect for HCPs and Patients	Treat HCPs and patients with respect and prioritize their well-being.
Conflict of Interest Management	Identify and manage potential conflicts of interest.
Fair Competition	Engage in fair competition and focus on product strengths.
Continuous Training and Development	Provide ongoing training on ethical practices and industry regulations.

Building Trust and Credibility with Healthcare Providers and Customers

Trust and credibility are critical for establishing and maintaining strong relationships with HCPs and customers. Sarah focused on building these through consistent, ethical practices and transparent communication.

Strategies for Building Trust and Credibility:

1. **Consistent and Reliable Communication:**
   - Ensure that all communications are consistent and reliable. Follow up on commitments and provide timely updates.
   - Use CRM systems to track interactions and ensure that information is accurately recorded and shared.

2. **Delivering Value:**
   - Focus on delivering value to HCPs and customers through educational resources, support services, and relevant information.
   - Offer solutions that address their specific needs and challenges.

3. **Engagement and Collaboration:**

- Engage HCPs and customers in meaningful dialogue and collaboration. Involve them in product development, research, and feedback processes.
- Show appreciation for their input and incorporate their suggestions into your strategies.

4. **Ethical Marketing Practices:**
   - Adhere to ethical marketing practices by ensuring that all promotional materials are truthful, balanced, and compliant with regulations.
   - Avoid any form of coercion or undue influence in marketing activities.

5. **Transparency in Pricing and Policies:**
   - Be transparent about pricing, discounts, and policies. Ensure that HCPs and customers understand the terms and conditions of any agreements.
   - Avoid hidden fees or complex terms that could lead to misunderstandings.

Example of Building Trust and Credibility:

Sarah's team developed a comprehensive engagement plan that included regular check-ins with HCPs, personalized educational webinars, and collaborative research initiatives. They used Salesforce to track interactions and ensure that all communications were consistent and reliable. Feedback from HCPs was actively sought and used to improve products and services.

Strategy	Description
Consistent and Reliable Communication	Ensure all communications are consistent and reliable.
Delivering Value	Provide educational resources, support services, and relevant information.
Engagement and Collaboration	Engage HCPs and customers in meaningful dialogue and collaboration.
Ethical Marketing Practices	Ensure promotional materials are truthful and compliant with regulations.

Transparency in Pricing and Policies	Be transparent about pricing, discounts, and policies.

Integrating Compliance and Ethics into Daily Operations

Integrating compliance and ethical considerations into daily operations ensures that these principles become a natural part of the team's workflow.

Steps to Integrate Compliance and Ethics:

1. **Policy Development and Communication:**
   - Develop clear policies on compliance and ethics. Ensure that these policies are communicated effectively to all team members.
   - Include examples and case studies to illustrate the application of these policies.

2. **Regular Training and Refresher Courses:**
   - Provide regular training and refresher courses on compliance and ethics. Ensure that new team members receive comprehensive onboarding on these topics.
   - Use interactive training methods, such as workshops and role-playing, to engage participants.

3. **Monitoring and Auditing:**
   - Implement monitoring and auditing processes to ensure adherence to compliance and ethical standards.
   - Conduct regular reviews and audits to identify any areas of concern and address them promptly.

4. **Leadership Commitment:**
   - Ensure that leadership demonstrates a strong commitment to compliance and ethics. Lead by example and reinforce the importance of these principles.
   - Recognize and reward team members who uphold high ethical standards.

5. **Reporting Mechanisms:**
   - Establish clear reporting mechanisms for ethical concerns and compliance issues. Ensure that team members feel comfortable reporting any concerns without fear of retaliation.
   - Address reported issues promptly and transparently.

Example of Integration:

Sarah's team developed a comprehensive compliance and ethics policy manual, which was distributed to all team members. They conducted quarterly training sessions and annual refresher courses. An internal audit system was set up to monitor compliance, and an ethics hotline was established for anonymous reporting. Leadership actively participated in training sessions and demonstrated their commitment to ethical practices.

Step	Description
Policy Development and Communication	Develop clear policies and communicate them effectively.
Regular Training and Refresher Courses	Provide ongoing training and refresher courses on compliance and ethics.
Monitoring and Auditing	Implement processes to monitor and audit compliance and ethics.
Leadership Commitment	Ensure leadership demonstrates a strong commitment to these principles.
Reporting Mechanisms	Establish clear mechanisms for reporting ethical concerns and compliance issues.

Conclusion

As Sarah J. reflected on the journey of transforming her pharmaceutical sales team, she recognized that maintaining ethical standards and ensuring compliance were crucial for long-term success. By understanding industry regulations, ensuring ethical practices in sales activities, and building trust and credibility, they were able to establish strong relationships with HCPs and customers.

The lessons learned in this chapter highlight the importance of integrating compliance and ethics into daily operations, fostering a culture of transparency and integrity, and continuously striving to improve. These principles are essential for any sales team in the pharmaceutical industry, ensuring that they not only achieve their business goals but also contribute positively to the healthcare community.

With a strong foundation in compliance and ethics, Sarah and her team were well-equipped to navigate the complexities of the pharmaceutical industry and continue making a lasting impact on the healthcare providers and patients they served.

Chapter 11: Driving Continuous Improvement and Innovation

Introduction

With a strong foundation in place, Sarah J. and her pharmaceutical sales team had achieved remarkable success. However, Sarah understood that sustaining this success required a commitment to continuous improvement and a culture of innovation. This chapter explores how Sarah fostered an environment where her team could continuously improve, innovate, and adapt to the ever-evolving pharmaceutical landscape. Building on the previous chapters, this chapter highlights the strategies, practices, and mindsets that drove their ongoing success.

Fostering a Culture of Continuous Improvement

Continuous improvement is the ongoing effort to enhance products, services, and processes. For Sarah and her team, this meant regularly assessing their strategies, identifying areas for improvement, and implementing changes to achieve better outcomes.

Key Strategies for Continuous Improvement:

1. **Regular Feedback and Evaluation:**
   - Implement regular feedback mechanisms, such as surveys, performance reviews, and one-on-one meetings, to gather insights from team members and HCPs.
   - Use this feedback to evaluate current practices and identify areas for improvement.

2. **Data-Driven Decision Making:**
   - Leverage data analytics tools like Tableau to analyze performance metrics, customer interactions, and market trends.
   - Make data-driven decisions to optimize sales strategies and improve customer engagement.

3. **Process Optimization:**
   - Continuously assess and refine sales processes to enhance efficiency and effectiveness.
   - Implement lean principles to eliminate waste and streamline operations.

4. **Professional Development:**

- Invest in ongoing training and development programs to enhance the skills and knowledge of the sales team.
- Encourage team members to pursue certifications, attend workshops, and participate in industry conferences.

Example of Continuous Improvement Implementation:
Sarah established a monthly review process where the team analyzed performance data and discussed feedback from HCPs. They used Tableau to visualize trends and identify areas for improvement. Based on these insights, they optimized their sales processes and implemented targeted training programs to address skill gaps.

Strategy	Description
Regular Feedback and Evaluation	Implement feedback mechanisms to gather insights and evaluate practices.
Data-Driven Decision Making	Use data analytics to make informed decisions and optimize strategies.
Process Optimization	Assess and refine sales processes for efficiency and effectiveness.
Professional Development	Invest in ongoing training and development programs.

Embracing Innovation

Innovation is crucial for staying competitive in the pharmaceutical industry. Sarah encouraged her team to embrace innovative ideas and technologies to drive growth and improve customer experiences.

Key Strategies for Embracing Innovation:
1. **Encouraging Creativity:**
    - Foster a culture where team members feel empowered to share their ideas and think creatively.
    - Create innovation hubs or brainstorming sessions to explore new concepts and solutions.
2. **Adopting New Technologies:**

- Stay updated on the latest technological advancements and assess their potential impact on the sales process.
- Implement new tools and platforms that enhance efficiency, customer engagement, and data analysis.

3. **Collaborative Innovation:**
   - Encourage collaboration with other departments, such as marketing, R&D, and IT, to leverage diverse perspectives and expertise.
   - Engage with external partners, such as technology providers and academic institutions, to drive innovation.

4. **Piloting and Scaling:**
   - Pilot new ideas and technologies on a small scale to test their feasibility and effectiveness.
   - Scale successful pilots across the organization to maximize impact.

Example of Innovation Implementation:

Sarah introduced a quarterly innovation challenge where team members pitched new ideas for improving sales processes and customer engagement. One successful idea was the implementation of a virtual reality (VR) platform for product demonstrations. After a successful pilot, the VR platform was rolled out to the entire sales team, enhancing their ability to engage with HCPs.

Strategy	Description
Encouraging Creativity	Foster a culture of creativity and idea sharing.
Adopting New Technologies	Implement tools and platforms that enhance efficiency and engagement.
Collaborative Innovation	Collaborate with other departments and external partners to drive innovation.
Piloting and Scaling	Pilot new ideas and technologies and scale successful pilots across the organization.

Developing a Resilient and Adaptive Team

In an industry characterized by rapid changes and uncertainties, resilience and adaptability are essential traits for any sales team. Sarah focused on developing these qualities within her team to ensure they could thrive in any environment.

Key Strategies for Building Resilience and Adaptability:

1. **Resilience Training:**
   - Provide training on resilience, stress management, and mental health to help team members cope with challenges and setbacks.
   - Encourage a positive mindset and the ability to bounce back from failures.

2. **Adaptive Leadership:**
   - Model adaptive leadership by being flexible and open to change. Demonstrate how to navigate uncertainty and make decisions in dynamic environments.
   - Empower team members to take initiative and make decisions within their areas of responsibility.

3. **Scenario Planning:**
   - Conduct scenario planning exercises to prepare for potential disruptions and changes in the market.
   - Develop contingency plans and ensure the team is ready to adapt to different scenarios.

4. **Continuous Learning:**
   - Foster a culture of continuous learning where team members are encouraged to stay updated on industry trends and best practices.
   - Provide access to resources such as online courses, industry publications, and networking opportunities.

Example of Resilience and Adaptability Implementation:

Sarah implemented resilience training workshops and encouraged her team to practice mindfulness and stress management techniques. She also conducted scenario planning sessions to prepare for market changes, such as new regulations or competitor actions. This proactive approach helped the team stay resilient and adaptive in the face of challenges.

Strategy	Description
Resilience Training	Provide training on resilience, stress management, and mental health.

Adaptive Leadership	Model flexibility and empower team members to navigate uncertainty.
Scenario Planning	Conduct exercises to prepare for potential disruptions and develop contingency plans.
Continuous Learning	Foster a culture of continuous learning and provide access to resources.

Enhancing Customer-Centricity

A customer-centric approach is vital for building strong relationships and delivering value to HCPs and patients. Sarah reinforced the importance of putting customers at the center of their strategies and actions.

Key Strategies for Enhancing Customer-Centricity:

1. **Deepening Customer Insights:**
   - Use CRM systems and data analytics to gather and analyze customer data, preferences, and feedback.
   - Develop detailed customer personas to guide personalized engagement strategies.

2. **Personalized Customer Experiences:**
   - Tailor interactions and communications based on individual customer needs and preferences.
   - Use digital marketing tools to create personalized content and campaigns that resonate with customers.

3. **Proactive Customer Engagement:**
   - Engage with customers proactively by anticipating their needs and providing timely solutions.
   - Implement regular check-ins and follow-ups to maintain strong relationships and address any concerns.

4. **Customer Feedback Loop:**
   - Establish a robust feedback loop to gather customer insights and use them to improve products, services, and processes.
   - Act on feedback and communicate any changes or improvements to customers.

Example of Customer-Centricity Implementation:

Sarah's team used Salesforce CRM to develop detailed customer personas and track interactions. They implemented HubSpot to create personalized email campaigns and content tailored to the needs of different HCP segments. Regular check-ins and follow-ups ensured that the team stayed connected with customers and addressed their needs proactively.

Strategy	Description
Deepening Customer Insights	Use CRM systems and data analytics to gather and analyze customer data.
Personalized Customer Experiences	Tailor interactions and communications based on individual needs.
Proactive Customer Engagement	Engage with customers proactively and anticipate their needs.
Customer Feedback Loop	Establish a feedback loop to gather insights and improve products and services.

Measuring and Celebrating Success

To sustain motivation and drive continuous improvement, it is important to measure success and celebrate achievements. Sarah implemented a comprehensive performance measurement system and ensured that successes were recognized and celebrated.

Key Strategies for Measuring and Celebrating Success:

1. **Performance Metrics:**
   - Establish clear performance metrics to track individual and team progress towards goals.
   - Use data analytics to monitor key indicators such as sales performance, customer satisfaction, and engagement levels.

2. **Regular Performance Reviews:**
   - Conduct regular performance reviews to assess progress, provide feedback, and identify areas for improvement.
   - Use these reviews to set new goals and action plans.

3. **Recognition and Rewards:**
   - Implement a recognition and rewards program to celebrate individual and team achievements.
   - Recognize contributions through awards, bonuses, and public acknowledgment.

4. **Team Celebrations:**
   - Organize team celebrations to mark major milestones and successes. Use these events to build camaraderie and reinforce a positive team culture.
   - Share success stories and lessons learned to inspire and motivate the team.

Example of Measuring and Celebrating Success:

Sarah's team used Salesforce and Tableau to track performance metrics and monitor progress. They conducted quarterly performance reviews and set new goals based on the insights gained. A recognition program was implemented to celebrate top performers, and team celebrations were held to mark major achievements and build team spirit.

Strategy	Description
Performance Metrics	Establish clear metrics to track progress towards goals.
Regular Performance Reviews	Conduct reviews to assess progress, provide feedback, and set new goals.
Recognition and Rewards	Implement a program to celebrate individual and team achievements.
Team Celebrations	Organize events to mark milestones and build camaraderie.

Conclusion

As Sarah J. reflected on the journey of continuous improvement and innovation, she felt confident that her team was well-equipped to navigate the ever-changing pharmaceutical landscape. By fostering a culture of continuous improvement, embracing innovation, developing resilience and adaptability, enhancing customer-centricity, and measuring and celebrating success, they had built a strong foundation for sustained success.

The lessons learned in this chapter highlight the importance of a proactive and dynamic approach to sales management. By continuously striving to improve and innovate, Sarah and her team were able to stay ahead of the competition and deliver exceptional value to their customers and patients.

With these principles in place, Sarah looked forward to the future with optimism and determination. She knew that their commitment to excellence, integrity, and customer-centricity would continue to drive their success and make a positive impact on the healthcare community.

Chapter 12: Navigating Future Challenges and Opportunities

Introduction

As Sarah J. reflected on the numerous achievements and transformations her team had experienced, she knew that the journey of innovation and improvement was far from over. The pharmaceutical industry is dynamic and ever-changing, and staying ahead requires continuous adaptation and strategic foresight. In this chapter, we explore the future challenges and opportunities that lie ahead for Sarah and her team. We will delve into the strategies and mindsets needed to navigate these challenges and seize opportunities to sustain growth and drive further success.

Embracing Digital Transformation

The digital revolution continues to reshape industries globally, and the pharmaceutical sector is no exception. Embracing digital transformation is crucial for staying competitive and delivering value in a rapidly evolving market.

Key Areas of Digital Transformation:

1. **Advanced Data Analytics:**
   - Utilize advanced data analytics to gain deeper insights into customer behavior, market trends, and operational efficiency.
   - Implement predictive analytics to anticipate future trends and make proactive decisions.

2. **Artificial Intelligence and Machine Learning:**
   - Leverage AI and machine learning to optimize sales strategies, personalize customer interactions, and improve decision-making.
   - Use AI-powered tools for predictive modeling, demand forecasting, and customer segmentation.

3. **Digital Marketing and Engagement:**
   - Enhance digital marketing strategies by leveraging social media, content marketing, and email campaigns to engage with HCPs and customers.

- Implement omnichannel marketing approaches to deliver a seamless and personalized customer experience across various platforms.
4. **Telehealth and Remote Engagement:**
   - Embrace telehealth and remote engagement tools to connect with HCPs and patients, especially in light of the increased demand for virtual interactions.
   - Use telehealth platforms to conduct virtual meetings, product demonstrations, and educational sessions.

Example of Digital Transformation Implementation:

Sarah's team adopted AI-powered tools like IBM Watson to analyze large datasets and gain actionable insights. They also implemented a comprehensive digital marketing strategy using platforms like HubSpot and Hootsuite to manage social media campaigns and email marketing. Additionally, they integrated telehealth solutions to facilitate remote engagement with HCPs.

Area	Description
Advanced Data Analytics	Utilize advanced analytics for deeper insights and proactive decision-making.
Artificial Intelligence and Machine Learning	Leverage AI and machine learning to optimize strategies and personalize interactions.
Digital Marketing and Engagement	Enhance marketing strategies through social media, content marketing, and email campaigns.
Telehealth and Remote Engagement	Embrace telehealth tools for virtual interactions with HCPs and patients.

Adapting to Regulatory Changes

The pharmaceutical industry is subject to stringent regulations that continuously evolve. Staying compliant and adapting to regulatory changes is critical for maintaining credibility and avoiding legal pitfalls.

Key Strategies for Adapting to Regulatory Changes:

1. **Proactive Monitoring:**

- Stay informed about regulatory changes and updates from bodies like the FDA, EMA, and other national regulatory agencies.
- Subscribe to industry newsletters, attend regulatory conferences, and participate in professional networks.

2. **Compliance Training:**
   - Provide regular compliance training to ensure that all team members are aware of the latest regulations and best practices.
   - Use real-world scenarios and case studies to illustrate the application of compliance principles.

3. **Policy Updates and Audits:**
   - Regularly review and update company policies to align with new regulations.
   - Conduct internal audits to ensure compliance and identify areas for improvement.

4. **Collaboration with Legal and Regulatory Experts:**
   - Work closely with legal and regulatory experts to navigate complex regulatory landscapes.
   - Seek their guidance on interpreting regulations and implementing compliant practices.

Example of Adapting to Regulatory Changes:

Sarah's team implemented a proactive monitoring system to stay updated on regulatory changes. They collaborated with regulatory experts to update their policies and conducted quarterly compliance training sessions. Regular audits ensured adherence to regulations, and any issues were promptly addressed.

Strategy	Description
Proactive Monitoring	Stay informed about regulatory changes through newsletters, conferences, and networks.
Compliance Training	Provide regular training using real-world scenarios and case studies.
Policy Updates and Audits	Regularly review and update policies, and conduct internal audits.

Collaboration with Experts	Work closely with legal and regulatory experts for guidance and compliance.

Enhancing Customer-Centric Innovation

Innovation that centers around customer needs and preferences is key to staying relevant and competitive. Sarah focused on fostering customer-centric innovation to deliver superior value and improve patient outcomes.

Key Strategies for Customer-Centric Innovation:

1. **Customer Feedback Integration:**
   - Actively seek and integrate feedback from HCPs and patients to inform product development and service improvements.
   - Use surveys, focus groups, and social media listening tools to gather insights.

2. **Collaborative Innovation:**
   - Partner with HCPs, patients, and other stakeholders to co-create solutions that address real-world challenges.
   - Engage in collaborative research and development projects to leverage diverse perspectives.

3. **Personalized Solutions:**
   - Develop personalized solutions that cater to the specific needs and preferences of different customer segments.
   - Use data analytics to identify trends and tailor products and services accordingly.

4. **Agile Development:**
   - Implement agile development methodologies to rapidly prototype, test, and refine innovative ideas.
   - Encourage a fail-fast approach to quickly identify and iterate on promising solutions.

Example of Customer-Centric Innovation:

Sarah's team launched an initiative to gather extensive feedback from HCPs and patients using tools like SurveyMonkey and social media listening platforms. They partnered with key opinion leaders (KOLs) and patient advocacy groups to co-create new product features. Agile development methodologies were used to bring these innovations to market quickly.

Strategy	Description
Customer Feedback Integration	Actively seek and integrate feedback from HCPs and patients.
Collaborative Innovation	Partner with stakeholders to co-create solutions and engage in collaborative R&D.
Personalized Solutions	Develop solutions tailored to the needs of different customer segments.
Agile Development	Use agile methodologies to rapidly prototype, test, and refine ideas.

Strengthening Relationships with Key Stakeholders

Building and maintaining strong relationships with key stakeholders, including HCPs, patients, regulatory bodies, and partners, is essential for long-term success.

Key Strategies for Strengthening Stakeholder Relationships:

1. **Transparent Communication:**
   - Maintain open and transparent communication with all stakeholders.
   - Regularly update stakeholders on company developments, product updates, and regulatory changes.

2. **Collaborative Partnerships:**
   - Develop collaborative partnerships with HCPs, academic institutions, and industry organizations.
   - Engage in joint research projects, clinical trials, and educational initiatives.

3. **Stakeholder Engagement Programs:**
   - Implement stakeholder engagement programs to foster long-term relationships and mutual trust.
   - Organize workshops, seminars, and conferences to facilitate knowledge exchange and collaboration.

4. **Patient Advocacy:**
   - Partner with patient advocacy groups to better understand patient needs and improve patient care.
   - Support initiatives that promote patient education, awareness, and empowerment.

Example of Strengthening Stakeholder Relationships:

Sarah's team established a stakeholder engagement program that included regular updates, collaborative research projects, and educational initiatives. They partnered with academic institutions for clinical trials and supported patient advocacy groups through sponsorships and joint campaigns. Transparent communication was maintained through newsletters and webinars.

Strategy	Description
Transparent Communication	Maintain open communication and regularly update stakeholders.
Collaborative Partnerships	Develop partnerships with HCPs, academic institutions, and industry organizations.
Stakeholder Engagement Programs	Implement programs to foster long-term relationships and trust.
Patient Advocacy	Partner with patient advocacy groups to understand and support patient needs.

Navigating Global Market Challenges

Expanding into global markets presents unique challenges and opportunities. Sarah focused on understanding and navigating these challenges to drive international growth.

Key Strategies for Navigating Global Market Challenges:

1. **Market Research and Analysis:**
   - Conduct thorough market research to understand the regulatory, cultural, and economic landscape of target markets.
   - Analyze competitive dynamics and identify market entry opportunities.

2. **Localized Strategies:**
   - Develop localized marketing and sales strategies that resonate with the specific needs and preferences of each market.
   - Adapt product offerings, messaging, and promotional activities to align with local regulations and cultural nuances.

3. **Global Partnerships:**

- Establish strategic partnerships with local distributors, healthcare organizations, and regulatory bodies.
- Leverage local expertise to navigate regulatory requirements and market dynamics.

4. **Supply Chain Optimization:**
   - Optimize the supply chain to ensure efficient and reliable delivery of products to global markets.
   - Implement robust logistics and distribution networks to minimize disruptions.

Example of Navigating Global Market Challenges:

Sarah's team conducted extensive market research to understand the regulatory and cultural landscape of target markets in Asia and Europe. They developed localized marketing campaigns and adapted their product offerings to meet local needs. Strategic partnerships were established with local distributors and healthcare organizations to facilitate market entry and compliance.

Strategy	Description
Market Research and Analysis	Conduct thorough research to understand target markets.
Localized Strategies	Develop strategies tailored to the needs of each market.
Global Partnerships	Establish partnerships with local entities to navigate market dynamics.
Supply Chain Optimization	Optimize logistics and distribution networks for global markets.

Fostering a Culture of Diversity and Inclusion

A diverse and inclusive workforce brings a wealth of perspectives and ideas, driving innovation and improving decision-making. Sarah emphasized the importance of fostering a culture of diversity and inclusion within her team.

Key Strategies for Fostering Diversity and Inclusion:

1. **Inclusive Hiring Practices:**
   - Implement inclusive hiring practices to attract and retain a diverse talent pool.
   - Use blind recruitment techniques and diverse interview panels to minimize bias.

2. **Diversity Training and Awareness:**

- Provide regular training on diversity, equity, and inclusion to raise awareness and promote understanding.
- Encourage open discussions about diversity and inclusion to foster a supportive environment.

3. **Employee Resource Groups (ERGs):**
   - Establish ERGs to support employees from diverse backgrounds and provide a platform for networking and advocacy.
   - Empower ERGs to lead initiatives that promote diversity and inclusion within the organization.

4. **Mentorship and Sponsorship Programs:**
   - Implement mentorship and sponsorship programs to support the development and advancement of underrepresented employees.
   - Pair mentors and sponsors with mentees to provide guidance, support, and opportunities for growth.

Example of Fostering Diversity and Inclusion:

Sarah's team implemented inclusive hiring practices and provided regular diversity training sessions. They established ERGs focused on various aspects of diversity, such as gender, ethnicity, and LGBTQ+ inclusion. Mentorship programs were introduced to support the career development of underrepresented employees, fostering a culture of inclusivity and empowerment.

Strategy	Description
Inclusive Hiring Practices	Implement practices to attract and retain a diverse talent pool.
Diversity Training and Awareness	Provide training to raise awareness and promote understanding.
Employee Resource Groups (ERGs)	Establish ERGs to support diverse employees and lead initiatives.
Mentorship and Sponsorship Programs	Implement programs to support the development of underrepresented employees.

Investing in Sustainability and Corporate Social Responsibility (CSR)

Sustainability and CSR are increasingly important in the pharmaceutical industry. Sarah prioritized these areas to ensure that her team contributed positively to society and the environment.

Key Strategies for Sustainability and CSR:

1. **Sustainable Practices:**
   - Implement sustainable practices in manufacturing, packaging, and distribution to minimize environmental impact.
   - Use eco-friendly materials and reduce waste through recycling and efficient resource management.

2. **Community Engagement:**
   - Engage with local communities through volunteer programs, educational initiatives, and health awareness campaigns.
   - Support local healthcare facilities and provide resources to improve community health.

3. **Ethical Sourcing:**
   - Ensure that all materials and ingredients are sourced ethically and sustainably.
   - Partner with suppliers who adhere to ethical and environmental standards.

4. **Transparency and Reporting:**
   - Maintain transparency in CSR and sustainability efforts by regularly reporting on progress and impact.
   - Use frameworks like the Global Reporting Initiative (GRI) to standardize reporting and ensure accountability.

Example of Investing in Sustainability and CSR:

Sarah's team implemented sustainable practices in their operations, such as using eco-friendly packaging and reducing waste. They engaged with local communities through health awareness campaigns and volunteer programs. Ethical sourcing policies were established to ensure that all materials met high ethical and environmental standards. Regular CSR reports were published to maintain transparency and accountability.

Strategy	Description
Sustainable Practices	Implement eco-friendly practices in manufacturing, packaging, and distribution.

Community Engagement	Engage with local communities through volunteer programs and health initiatives.
Ethical Sourcing	Ensure materials and ingredients are sourced ethically and sustainably.
Transparency and Reporting	Maintain transparency through regular CSR reporting.

Embracing the Future with Confidence

As Sarah J. looked towards the future, she felt a sense of confidence and optimism. The strategies and practices her team had implemented positioned them well to navigate future challenges and seize new opportunities. By embracing digital transformation, adapting to regulatory changes, enhancing customer-centric innovation, strengthening stakeholder relationships, navigating global markets, fostering diversity and inclusion, and investing in sustainability and CSR, they were well-prepared to continue their journey of success and impact.

Final Reflections:

1. **Commitment to Continuous Improvement:**
   - Sarah recognized that continuous improvement was a never-ending journey. She committed to regularly assessing and refining their strategies to stay ahead in the industry.

2. **Focus on Innovation:**
   - Embracing innovation was essential for staying competitive. Sarah encouraged her team to think creatively and explore new ideas to drive growth and enhance customer experiences.

3. **Customer-Centric Approach:**
   - Putting customers at the center of their strategies ensured that they delivered value and built strong relationships. Sarah emphasized the importance of understanding and addressing customer needs.

4. **Ethical and Responsible Practices:**
   - Maintaining ethical and responsible practices was critical for building trust and credibility. Sarah committed to upholding high standards of integrity and compliance.

5. **Empowerment and Inclusion:**
   - Empowering and including all team members fostered a supportive and innovative environment. Sarah focused on creating a culture where everyone could thrive.
6. **Sustainable and Socially Responsible:**
   - Investing in sustainability and CSR demonstrated their commitment to making a positive impact on society and the environment. Sarah prioritized these areas to ensure long-term success and responsibility.

As Sarah and her team continued their journey, they remained dedicated to their vision of improving patient outcomes and making a difference in the healthcare community. With a solid foundation in place and a forward-thinking mindset, they were ready to embrace the future with confidence and drive meaningful change.

Chapter 13: Conclusion and Future Outlook

Introduction

As Sarah J. sat down to reflect on her journey as a sales manager in the pharmaceutical industry, she realized how much she and her team had accomplished. From building a customer-centric culture to navigating ethical considerations and embracing continuous improvement, each step was a testament to their resilience and dedication. This chapter recaps the key concepts and strategies discussed in previous chapters, explores the future of pharmaceutical sales management, and emphasizes the importance of continuous learning and development.

Recap of Key Concepts and Strategies

Over the course of this book, we have delved into numerous strategies and practices that have helped Sarah and her team achieve success. Let's recap the key concepts and strategies that have been instrumental in their journey:

1. **Visionary Leadership and Strategic Planning:**
   - Sarah's ability to articulate a clear vision and develop strategic plans guided her team's efforts and kept them aligned with their goals.

2. **Customer-Centric Culture:**
   - By placing customers at the center of their strategies, Sarah's team was able to deliver value, build strong relationships, and improve patient outcomes.

3. **Ethical Practices and Compliance:**
   - Maintaining ethical standards and ensuring compliance with industry regulations were crucial for building trust and credibility with healthcare providers (HCPs) and customers.

4. **Continuous Improvement and Innovation:**
   - Embracing a culture of continuous improvement and innovation allowed Sarah's team to stay ahead of the competition and adapt to changing market dynamics.

5. **Resilience and Adaptability:**

- Developing resilience and adaptability within the team ensured they could navigate challenges and uncertainties effectively.

6. **Leveraging Technology:**
   - Utilizing advanced technologies, such as AI, data analytics, and digital collaboration tools, enhanced decision-making, efficiency, and customer engagement.

7. **Building Strong Stakeholder Relationships:**
   - Fostering strong relationships with key stakeholders, including HCPs, patients, regulatory bodies, and partners, was essential for long-term success.

8. **Diversity and Inclusion:**
   - Promoting diversity and inclusion within the team brought diverse perspectives and ideas, driving innovation and improving decision-making.

9. **Sustainability and Corporate Social Responsibility (CSR):**
   - Investing in sustainability and CSR demonstrated the team's commitment to making a positive impact on society and the environment.

The Future of Pharmaceutical Sales Management

The pharmaceutical industry is continuously evolving, and the future of sales management will be shaped by several key trends and developments. Here's a look at what lies ahead:

1. **Digital Transformation and Automation:**
   - The integration of digital technologies and automation will continue to revolutionize pharmaceutical sales. AI-powered tools will enhance data analysis, customer segmentation, and personalized marketing, while automation will streamline administrative tasks.

2. Personalized Customer Engagement:

- Personalized customer engagement will become increasingly important. Sales teams will leverage data-driven insights to tailor their interactions and provide HCPs and patients with relevant, timely information.

3. Virtual and Remote Interactions:

- The rise of telehealth and remote engagement will reshape how sales teams interact with HCPs and customers. Virtual meetings, webinars, and digital platforms will become standard practices for communication and education.

4. Regulatory and Ethical Considerations:

- As regulations continue to evolve, maintaining compliance and ethical standards will remain critical. Sales teams will need to stay informed about regulatory changes and ensure their practices align with industry guidelines.

5. Collaborative Partnerships:

- Collaborative partnerships with HCPs, academic institutions, and technology providers will drive innovation and enhance product development. Engaging in joint research projects and clinical trials will be essential for advancing healthcare solutions.

6. Sustainability and Social Impact:

- The focus on sustainability and social impact will grow. Pharmaceutical companies will need to demonstrate their commitment to environmental stewardship and social responsibility through sustainable practices and community engagement.

7. **Agile and Adaptive Leadership:**
   - Agile and adaptive leadership will be crucial for navigating the complexities of the pharmaceutical industry. Leaders will need to foster a culture of innovation, resilience, and continuous learning to stay competitive.

Continuing Your Journey of Learning and Development

The journey of learning and development is ongoing, and staying ahead in the pharmaceutical industry requires a commitment to continuous growth. Here are some strategies to help you continue your journey:

1. **Stay Informed:**
   - Keep up with industry trends, regulatory updates, and technological advancements. Subscribe to industry publications, attend conferences, and participate in professional networks to stay informed.

2. **Invest in Professional Development:**
   - Pursue certifications, attend workshops, and enroll in online courses to enhance your skills and knowledge. Continuous professional development will help you stay competitive and adapt to industry changes.

3. **Foster a Growth Mindset:**
   - Embrace a growth mindset by viewing challenges as opportunities for learning and improvement. Encourage your team to take risks, experiment with new ideas, and learn from failures.

4. **Leverage Technology:**
   - Utilize advanced technologies to enhance your learning and development efforts. Use e-learning platforms, virtual reality simulations, and AI-driven tools to gain new insights and skills.

5. **Engage in Mentorship:**
   - Seek out mentors who can provide guidance, support, and valuable insights. Additionally, consider mentoring

others to share your knowledge and help them grow in their careers.

6. **Participate in Collaborative Projects:**
    - Engage in collaborative projects with peers, academic institutions, and industry organizations. Collaborative efforts can lead to innovative solutions and provide valuable learning experiences.

7. **Reflect and Evaluate:**
    - Regularly reflect on your experiences and evaluate your progress. Identify areas for improvement and set new goals to continue growing and developing.

8. **Cultivate a Learning Culture:**
    - Foster a culture of continuous learning within your team. Encourage open discussions, knowledge sharing, and ongoing education to ensure everyone is aligned and motivated to grow.

Example of Continuing Learning and Development:

Sarah prioritized her professional development by enrolling in advanced leadership courses and attending industry conferences. She also encouraged her team to pursue certifications and participate in workshops. Regular team meetings were held to discuss industry trends, share knowledge, and identify opportunities for improvement.

Strategy	Description
Stay Informed	Keep up with industry trends, regulatory updates, and technological advancements.
Invest in Professional Development	Pursue certifications, workshops, and online courses.
Foster a Growth Mindset	Embrace challenges as opportunities for learning and improvement.
Leverage Technology	Utilize e-learning platforms, virtual reality simulations, and AI-driven tools.
Engage in Mentorship	Seek out mentors and consider mentoring others.
Participate in Collaborative Projects	Engage in projects with peers, academic institutions, and industry organizations.

Reflect and Evaluate	Regularly reflect on experiences and set new goals.
Cultivate a Learning Culture	Foster a culture of continuous learning within the team.

Conclusion

As Sarah J. looked back on her journey and the progress her team had made, she felt a deep sense of pride and accomplishment. They had navigated numerous challenges, embraced innovation, and fostered a culture of continuous improvement and ethical responsibility. The future of pharmaceutical sales management holds exciting opportunities and challenges, and Sarah was confident that her team was well-equipped to thrive.

By embracing digital transformation, adapting to regulatory changes, enhancing customer-centric innovation, and fostering strong stakeholder relationships, they had built a solid foundation for sustained success. The commitment to diversity, inclusion, sustainability, and continuous learning ensured that they remained agile and resilient in the face of change.

As you continue your journey in pharmaceutical sales management, remember that success is not just about achieving goals but about the continuous pursuit of excellence. Stay curious, embrace change, and never stop learning. By doing so, you will not only achieve your professional goals but also make a meaningful impact on the healthcare community and the lives of patients.

Final Reflections:

1. **Embrace Change:**
   - Change is constant in the pharmaceutical industry. Embrace it as an opportunity for growth and innovation.
2. **Focus on Customers:**
   - Keep customers at the center of your strategies. Understand their needs and deliver value through personalized solutions.
3. **Maintain Ethical Standards:**
   - Uphold high ethical standards and ensure compliance with industry regulations. Trust and credibility are key to long-term success.
4. **Foster Innovation:**

- Encourage creativity and innovation within your team. Explore new ideas and technologies to drive growth.

5. **Invest in Learning:**
   - Continuously invest in your learning and development. Stay informed, seek out new opportunities, and cultivate a growth mindset.

6. **Build Strong Relationships:**
   - Develop strong relationships with stakeholders, including HCPs, patients, and partners. Collaboration and trust are essential for success.

7. **Commit to Sustainability:**
   - Prioritize sustainability and social responsibility. Make a positive impact on society and the environment.

By integrating these principles into your daily operations and leadership approach, you will be well-prepared to navigate the complexities of the pharmaceutical industry and achieve lasting success.

Appendices

Appendix A: Templates and Checklists for Sales Managers

Template 1: Sales Strategy Plan

SECTION	DESCRIPTION
EXECUTIVE SUMMARY	Overview of the sales strategy, goals, and objectives.
MARKET ANALYSIS	Analysis of market trends, customer segments, and competitive landscape.
SALES GOALS	Specific, measurable sales targets for the period.
SALES TACTICS	Detailed tactics for achieving sales goals, including product positioning and messaging.
RESOURCE ALLOCATION	Allocation of resources, including budget, personnel, and technology.
PERFORMANCE METRICS	Key performance indicators (KPIs) to measure progress and success.
IMPLEMENTATION PLAN	Timeline and action plan for executing the sales strategy.

Template 2: Customer Engagement Plan

SECTION	DESCRIPTION
CUSTOMER PROFILE	Detailed profile of the target customer segment.
ENGAGEMENT OBJECTIVES	Specific objectives for engaging with the customer.
KEY MESSAGES	Core messages to communicate to the customer.
ENGAGEMENT CHANNELS	Channels to use for customer engagement (e.g., email, social media, face-to-face meetings).
ENGAGEMENT ACTIVITIES	Planned activities to engage the customer (e.g., webinars, product demos, educational content).
FOLLOW-UP PLAN	Plan for follow-up interactions and maintaining customer relationships.

Checklist 1: Sales Call Preparation

1. Research the customer's background and recent interactions.
2. Review the customer's current needs and challenges.
3. Prepare key messages and value propositions.
4. Identify potential objections and prepare responses.
5. Ensure all necessary materials (e.g., product brochures, presentations) are ready.
6. Set clear objectives for the call.
7. Confirm the meeting time and format (e.g., virtual, in-person).

Checklist 2: Post-Call Follow-Up

1. Send a thank-you email to the customer.
2. Summarize key points and agreements from the call.
3. Provide any additional information or materials requested by the customer.
4. Schedule the next follow-up interaction.
5. Update the CRM system with call details and next steps.
6. Review and adjust the engagement plan as needed.

Appendix B: Recommended Readings and Resources

Books:

1. **"The Challenger Sale: Taking Control of the Customer Conversation"** by Matthew Dixon and Brent Adamson
   - A groundbreaking approach to selling that emphasizes the importance of challenging customers' thinking and providing insights.
2. **"Sales Management. Simplified.: The Straight Truth About Getting Exceptional Results from Your Sales Team"** by Mike Weinberg
   - Practical advice on sales management, focusing on the fundamentals of leading a successful sales team.
3. **"SPIN Selling"** by Neil Rackham
   - A classic sales book that introduces the SPIN (Situation, Problem, Implication, Need-Payoff) selling technique, which is highly effective in complex sales environments.
4. **"The Lean Startup: How Today's Entrepreneurs Use Continuous Innovation to Create Radically Successful Businesses"** by Eric Ries

- A must-read for understanding how to implement agile and lean principles in your business operations.
5. **"Crucial Conversations: Tools for Talking When Stakes Are High"** by Kerry Patterson, Joseph Grenny, Ron McMillan, and Al Switzler
    - Techniques for effectively handling difficult conversations and improving communication skills.

Articles and Whitepapers:
1. **"The Future of Pharmaceutical Sales in the Digital Era"** by McKinsey & Company
    - Insights into how digital transformation is reshaping the pharmaceutical sales landscape.
2. **"Building Trust in the Pharmaceutical Industry"** by Deloitte
    - Strategies for maintaining trust and credibility with customers and stakeholders.
3. **"Personalizing Customer Experiences in Pharma"** by PwC
    - Best practices for creating personalized customer experiences in the pharmaceutical industry.
4. **"Navigating Regulatory Changes in Pharmaceuticals"** by EY
    - Guidance on adapting to regulatory changes and ensuring compliance in the pharmaceutical sector.

Online Resources and Courses:
1. **Coursera: Pharmaceutical Management**
    - Online courses covering various aspects of pharmaceutical management and sales.
2. **Harvard Business Review: Sales and Marketing**
    - Articles and resources on sales strategies, customer engagement, and leadership.
3. **PharmaVOICE**
    - An online platform offering articles, webinars, and industry news for pharmaceutical professionals.
4. **Salesforce Trailhead**
    - Free online training modules for mastering Salesforce CRM and improving sales effectiveness.

Appendix C: Glossary of Industry Terms

TERM	DEFINITION
AI (ARTIFICIAL INTELLIGENCE)	The simulation of human intelligence in machines programmed to think and learn like humans.
CRM (CUSTOMER RELATIONSHIP MANAGEMENT)	A technology for managing a company's interactions with current and potential customers.
FDA (FOOD AND DRUG ADMINISTRATION)	The U.S. agency responsible for regulating food, drugs, and medical devices.
HCP (HEALTHCARE PROVIDER)	Professionals who provide health care services to patients, such as doctors, nurses, and pharmacists.
KPI (KEY PERFORMANCE INDICATOR)	A measurable value that demonstrates how effectively a company is achieving key business objectives.
OMNICHANNEL MARKETING	An integrated approach that provides customers with a seamless experience across multiple channels.
PREDICTIVE ANALYTICS	The use of data, statistical algorithms, and machine learning techniques to identify the likelihood of future outcomes.
REGULATORY COMPLIANCE	Adherence to laws, regulations, guidelines, and specifications relevant to a business or industry.
TELEHEALTH	The use of digital information and communication technologies to access health care services remotely.
VIRTUAL REALITY (VR)	A simulated experience that can be similar to or completely different from the real world, used for

product demonstrations and training.

By utilizing these templates, checklists, readings, and understanding key industry terms, sales managers in the pharmaceutical industry can enhance their effectiveness and continue their journey of learning and development. These resources provide practical tools and knowledge to navigate the complexities of pharmaceutical sales management and drive sustained success.

References:

1. Food and Drug Administration (FDA). (n.d.). **New Drug Application (NDA)**. Retrieved from FDA Website
2. European Medicines Agency (EMA). (n.d.). **Marketing Authorisation**. Retrieved from EMA Website
3. Deloitte. (2021). **2021 Global Life Sciences Outlook**. Retrieved from Deloitte Website
4. McKinsey & Company. (2020). **Pharmaceuticals and Medical Products Practice**. Retrieved from McKinsey Website
5. McKinsey & Company. (2020). **Diversity Wins: How Inclusion Matters**. Retrieved from McKinsey Website
6. Deloitte. (2021). **2021 Global Human Capital Trends**. Retrieved from Deloitte Website
7. Harvard Business Review. (2016). **The Benefits of Inclusive Leadership**. Retrieved from HBR Website
8. Catalyst. (2021). **Why Diversity and Inclusion Matter: Quick Take**. Retrieved from [Catalyst Website](https://www.catalyst.org/research/why-diversity-and-in
9. Harvard Business Review. (2016). **The Benefits of Inclusive Leadership**. Retrieved from HBR Website
10. McKinsey & Company. (2020). **Diversity Wins: How Inclusion Matters**. Retrieved from McKinsey Website
11. Deloitte. (2021). **2021 Global Human Capital Trends**. Retrieved from Deloitte Website

12. Catalyst. (2021). **Why Diversity and Inclusion Matter: Quick Take**. Retrieved from Catalyst Website

13. Salesforce. (2020). **The Role of Technology in Enhancing Communication**. Retrieved from [Salesforce Website](https://www.sales

14. McKinsey & Company. (2020). **Diversity Wins: How Inclusion Matters**. Retrieved from McKinsey Website

15. Deloitte. (2021). **2021 Global Human Capital Trends**. Retrieved from Deloitte Website

16. Harvard Business Review. (2016). **The Benefits of Inclusive Leadership**. Retrieved from HBR Website

17. Salesforce. (2020). **The Role of Technology in Enhancing Communication**. Retrieved from Salesforce Website

18. Catalyst. (2021). **Why Diversity and Inclusion Matter: Quick Take**. Retrieved from Catalyst Website

19. Accenture. (2021). **Driving Digital Transformation in Pharmaceuticals**. Retrieved from Accenture Website

20. PwC. (2020). **Pharmaceuticals and Life Sciences Trends Report**. Retrieved from PwC Website

21. McKinsey & Company. (2020). **Diversity Wins: How Inclusion Matters**. Retrieved from McKinsey Website

22. Deloitte. (2021). **2021 Global Human Capital Trends**. Retrieved from Deloitte Website

23. Harvard Business Review. (2016). **The Benefits of Inclusive Leadership**. Retrieved from HBR Website

24. Salesforce. (2020). **The Role of Technology in Enhancing Communication**. Retrieved from Salesforce Website

25. Catalyst. (2021). **Why Diversity and Inclusion Matter: Quick Take**. Retrieved from Catalyst Website

26. Accenture. (2021). **Driving Digital Transformation in Pharmaceuticals**. Retrieved from Accenture Website

27. PwC. (2020). **Pharmaceuticals and Life Sciences Trends Report**. Retrieved from PwC Website

28. McKinsey & Company. (2020). **Diversity Wins: How Inclusion Matters**. Retrieved from McKinsey Website

29. Deloitte. (2021). **2021 Global Human Capital Trends**. Retrieved from Deloitte Website

30. Harvard Business Review. (2016). **The Benefits of Inclusive Leadership**. Retrieved from HBR Website

31. Salesforce. (2020). **The Role of Technology in Enhancing Communication**. Retrieved from Salesforce Website

32. Catalyst. (2021). **Why Diversity and Inclusion Matter: Quick Take**. Retrieved from Catalyst Website

33. Accenture. (2021). **Driving Digital Transformation in Pharmaceuticals**. Retrieved from Accenture Website

34. PwC. (2020). **Pharmaceuticals and Life Sciences Trends Report**. Retrieved from PwC Website

35. McKinsey & Company. (2020). **Diversity Wins: How Inclusion Matters**. Retrieved from McKinsey Website

36. Deloitte. (2021). **2021 Global Human Capital Trends**. Retrieved from Deloitte Website

37. Harvard Business Review. (2016). **The Benefits of Inclusive Leadership**. Retrieved from HBR Website

38. Salesforce. (2020). **The Role of Technology in Enhancing Communication**. Retrieved from Salesforce Website

39. Catalyst. (2021). **Why Diversity and Inclusion Matter: Quick Take**. Retrieved from Catalyst Website

40. Accenture. (2021). **Driving Digital Transformation in Pharmaceuticals**. Retrieved from Accenture Website

41. PwC. (2020). **Pharmaceuticals and Life Sciences Trends Report**. Retrieved from PwC Website

42. McKinsey & Company. (2020). **Diversity Wins: How Inclusion Matters**. Retrieved from McKinsey Website

43. Deloitte. (2021). **2021 Global Human Capital Trends**. Retrieved from Deloitte Website

44. Harvard Business Review. (2016). **The Benefits of Inclusive Leadership**. Retrieved from HBR Website

45. Salesforce. (2020). **The Role of Technology in Enhancing Communication**. Retrieved from Salesforce Website

46. Catalyst. (2021). **Why Diversity and Inclusion Matter: Quick Take**. Retrieved from Catalyst Website

47. Accenture. (2021). **Driving Digital Transformation in Pharmaceuticals**. Retrieved from Accenture Website

48. PwC. (2020). **Pharmaceuticals and Life Sciences Trends Report**. Retrieved from PwC Website

49. Salesforce. (2020). **The Role of Technology in Enhancing Communication**. Retrieved from Salesforce Website

50. HubSpot. (2021). **Digital Marketing Strategies for Pharmaceuticals**. Retrieved from HubSpot Website

51. Tableau. (2020). **Data Analytics for Informed Decision-Making**. Retrieved from Tableau Website

52. Zoom. (2020). **Enhancing Engagement through Virtual Meetings**. Retrieved from Zoom Website

53. Highspot. (2021). **Sales Enablement for Pharmaceuticals**. Retrieved from Highspot Website

54. Veeva Systems. (2020). **Mobile CRM for Real-Time Access**. Retrieved from Veeva Systems Website

55. Deloitte. (2021). **2021 Global Human Capital Trends**. Retrieved from Deloitte Website

56. Food and Drug Administration (FDA). (2021). **Guidance Documents**. Retrieved from FDA Website

57. European Medicines Agency (EMA). (2021). **Guidelines**. Retrieved from EMA Website

58. Department of Health and Human Services. (2021). **HIPAA Privacy Rule**. Retrieved from HHS Website

59. General Data Protection Regulation (GDPR). (2021). **Regulation (EU) 2016/679**. Retrieved from GDPR Website

60. Anti-Kickback Statute. (2021). **42 U.S.C. § 1320a-7b**. Retrieved from Office of Inspector General (OIG) Website

61. Bribery Act 2010. (2021). **Chapter 23**. Retrieved from UK Legislation Website

62. Salesforce. (2021). **CRM Best Practices for Sales Teams**. Retrieved from Salesforce Website

63. Tableau. (2020). **Using Data Analytics for Sales Optimization**. Retrieved from Tableau Website

64. Harvard Business Review. (2020). **The Importance of Continuous Improvement in Business**. Retrieved from HBR Website

65. HubSpot. (2021). **Personalizing Customer Experiences**. Retrieved from HubSpot Website

66. McKinsey & Company. (2020). **Building Resilience in Teams**. Retrieved from McKinsey Website

67. Deloitte. (2021). **Driving Innovation in Sales**. Retrieved from Deloitte Website

68. IBM Watson. (2021). **AI-Powered Tools for Data Analytics**. Retrieved from IBM Watson Website

69. HubSpot. (2021). **Comprehensive Digital Marketing Strategies**. Retrieved from HubSpot Website

70. Hootsuite. (2021). **Social Media Campaign Management**. Retrieved from Hootsuite Website

71. Global Reporting Initiative (GRI). (2021). **Sustainability Reporting Standards**. Retrieved from GRI Website

72. SurveyMonkey. (2021). **Customer Feedback Tools**. Retrieved from SurveyMonkey Website

73. McKinsey & Company. (2020). **Building Resilience in Teams**. Retrieved from McKinsey Website

74. Deloitte. (2021). **Driving Innovation in Sales**. Retrieved from Deloitte Website

75. IBM Watson. (2021). **AI-Powered Tools for Data Analytics**. Retrieved from IBM Watson Website

76. HubSpot. (2021). **Comprehensive Digital Marketing Strategies**. Retrieved from HubSpot Website

77. Hootsuite. (2021). **Social Media Campaign Management**. Retrieved from Hootsuite Website

78. Global Reporting Initiative (GRI). (2021). **Sustainability Reporting Standards**. Retrieved from GRI Website

79. SurveyMonkey. (2021). **Customer Feedback Tools**. Retrieved from SurveyMonkey Website

80. McKinsey & Company. (2020). **Building Resilience in Teams**. Retrieved from McKinsey Website

81. Deloitte. (2021). **Driving Innovation in Sales**. Retrieved from Deloitte Website

www.ingramcontent.com/pod-product-compliance
Lightning Source LLC
Chambersburg PA
CBHW052326220526
45472CB00001B/284